INTERVENTIONS

Conor Cunningham and Peter Candler

GENERAL EDITORS

It's not a question of whether one believes in God or not. Rather, it's a question of if, in the absence of God, we can have belief, any belief.

"If you live today," wrote Flannery O'Connor, "you breathe in nihilism." Whether "religious" or "secular," it is "the very gas you breathe." Both within and without the academy, there is an air common to both deconstruction and scientism — both might be described as species of *reductionism*. The dominance of these modes of knowledge in popular and professional discourse is quite incontestable, perhaps no more so where questions of theological import are often subjugated to the margins of intellectual respectability. Yet it is precisely the proponents and defenders of religious belief in an age of nihilism that are often among those most — unwittingly or not — complicit in this very reduction. In these latter cases, one frequently spies an accommodationist impulse, whereby our concepts must be first submitted to a prior philosophical court of appeal in order for them to render any intellectual value. To cite one particularly salient example, debates over the origins, nature, and ends of human life are routinely partitioned off into categories of "evolutionism" and "creationism," often with little nuance. Where attempts to mediate these arguments are to be found, frequently the strategy is that of a kind of accommodation: How can we adapt our belief in creation to an already established evolutionary metaphysic, or, how can we have our evolutionary cake and eat it too? It is sadly the case that, despite the best intentions of such "intellectual ecumenism," the distinctive voice of theology is the first one to succumb to aphony — either from impetuous overuse or from a deliberate silencing.

The books in this unique new series propose no such simple accommodation. They rather seek and perform tactical interventions in such debates in a manner that problematizes the accepted terms of such debates. They propose something altogether more demanding: through a kind of refusal of the disciplinary isolation now standard in modern universities, a genuinely interdisciplinary series of mediations of crucial concepts and key figures in contemporary thought. These volumes will attempt to discuss these topics as they are articulated within their own field, including their historical emergence, and cultural significance, which will provide a way into seemingly abstract discussions. At the same time, they aim to analyze what consequences such thinking may have for theology, both positive and negative, and, in light of these new perspectives, to develop an effective response — one that will better situate students of theology and professional theologians alike within the most vital debates informing Western society, and so increase their understanding of, participation in, and contribution to these.

To a generation brought up on a diet of deconstruction, on the one hand, and scientism, on the other, Interventions offers an alternative that is *otherwise than nihilistic* — doing so by approaching well-worn questions and topics, as well as historical and contemporary figures, from an original and interdisciplinary angle, and so avoid having to steer a course between the aforementioned Scylla and Charybdis.

This series will also seek to navigate not just through these twin dangers, but also through the dangerous "and" that joins them. That is to say, it will attempt to be genuinely interdisciplinary in avoiding the conjunctive approach to such topics that takes as paradigmatic a relationship of "theology and phenomenology" or "religion and science." Instead, the volumes in this series will, in general, attempt to treat such discourses not as discrete disciplines unto themselves, but as moments within a distended theological performance. Above all, they will hopefully contribute to a renewed atmosphere shared by theologians and philosophers (not to mention those in other disciplines) — an air that is not nothing.

CENTRE OF THEOLOGY AND PHILOSOPHY

(www.theologyphilosophycentre.co.uk)

Every doctrine which does not reach the one thing necessary, every separated philosophy, will remain deceived by false appearances. It will be a doctrine, it will not be Philosophy.

Maurice Blondel, 1861-1949

This book series is the product of the work carried out at the Centre of Theology and Philosophy (COTP), at the University of Nottingham.

The COTP is a research-led institution organized at the interstices of theology and philosophy. It is founded on the conviction that these two disciplines cannot be adequately understood or further developed, save with reference to each other. This is true in historical terms, since we cannot comprehend our Western cultural legacy unless we acknowledge the interaction of the Hebraic and Hellenic traditions. It is also true conceptually, since reasoning is not fully separable from faith and hope, or conceptual reflection from revelatory disclosure. The reverse also holds, in either case.

The Centre is concerned with:

- the historical interaction between theology and philosophy.
- the current relation between the two disciplines.
- attempts to overcome the analytic/continental divide in philosophy.
- the question of the status of "metaphysics": Is the term used equivocally? Is it now at an end? Or have twentieth-century attempts to have a postmetaphysical philosophy themselves come to an end?
- the construction of a rich Catholic humanism.

I am very glad to be associated with the endeavours of this extremely important Centre that helps to further work of enormous importance. Among its concerns is the question whether modernity is more an interim than a completion — an interim between a pre-modernity in which the porosity between theology and philosophy was granted, perhaps taken for granted, and a postmodernity where their porosity must be unclogged and enacted anew. Through the work of leading theologians of international stature and philosophers whose writings bear on this porosity, the Centre offers an exciting forum to advance in diverse ways this challenging and entirely needful, and cutting-edge work.

Professor William Desmond, Leuven

NATURALISM

Stewart Goetz & Charles Taliaferro

WILLIAM B. EERDMANS PUBLISHING COMPANY
GRAND RAPIDS, MICHIGAN / CAMBRIDGE, U.K.

Published 2008 by

Wm. B. Eerdmans Publishing Co.

2140 Oak Industrial Drive N.E., Grand Rapids, Michigan 49505 /

P.O. Box 163, Cambridge CB3 9PU U.K.

Printed in the United States of America

12 11 10 09 08   7 6 5 4 3 2 1

Library of Congress Cataloging-in-Publication Data

Goetz, Stewart.

Naturalism / Stewart Goetz & Charles Taliaferro.

p.   cm.   — (Interventions)

Includes bibliographical references.

ISBN 978-0-8028-0768-7 (pbk.: alk. paper)

1. Naturalism — Religious aspects — Christianity.

2. Apologetics.   I. Taliaferro, Charles.   II. Title.

BT1200.G64   2008

261.5'1 — dc22

2007046728

www.eerdmans.com

Contents

Acknowledgments

We are immensely grateful to Conor Cunningham for proposing this project, and for his sage advice. This book would not have been possible without the generous support of the John Templeton Foundation. We thank Tricia Little, Valerie Deal, Elizabeth Duel, Heather Kennon, and Mary Sotos for vital assistance. We also thank Mark Baker, Kelly Clark, Paul Copan, Robin Collins, Robert Hoveman, J. P. Moreland, and Dean Zimmerman for critical comments on an earlier version of this work. Stewart dedicates his contribution to this book to Carolyn with love, and Charles dedicates his portion to Jil Evans and to Christine and Stephen with love and gratitude for making evident Martin Buber's insight: "All real living is meeting."

Introduction

In this book we introduce and assess some of the leading forms of naturalism that are at the very center of contemporary philosophy. As will become apparent, the definition of "naturalism" is not a settled matter. In an important essay defending "a mature naturalism," Ernest Nagel observes: "The number of distinguishable doctrines for which the word 'naturalism' has been a counter in the history of thought is notorious" (Nagel 1958, 483). Despite the range of distinct versions of naturalism, those receiving the most recent philosophical and cultural attention provide a radical critique of our ordinary or commonplace understanding of ourselves and the world. Thus, Paul Churchland begins his book on naturalism with the following warning:

> You came to this book assuming that the basic units of human cognition are states such as thoughts, beliefs, perceptions, desires, and preferences. That assumption is natural enough: it is built into the vocabulary of every natural language.... These assumptions are central elements in our standard conception of human cognitive activity, a conception often called "folk psychology" to acknowledge it as the common property of folks generally. Their universality notwithstanding, these bedrock assumptions are probably mistaken. (Churchland 1995, 322)

Because so many powerful naturalist projects today do confront our standard understanding of ourselves, we thought it fitting to begin with a brief prelude on the standard or "folk" concept of human nature. After a modest sketch of our "bedrock assumptions," we then outline the competing schools of naturalism, highlighting the bearing these powerful philosophies have on our understanding of human nature, values, and the world.

Consider two recent articles from the *New York Times;* one is on the advantage of getting a good education, the other is on forming resolutions. We chose these articles largely because they reflect ordinary reasoning about interests and issues, and not because we believe that their main theses are true.

In "A Surprising Secret to a Long Life: Stay in School," Gina Kolata describes a variety of hypotheses about what it takes to live a long life: money, lack of stress, a loving family, and lots of friends. But what really matters? Apparently, the answer lies in education. James Smith, a health economist at the RAND Corporation, says that "what may make the biggest difference is keeping young people in school. A few extra years of school is associated with extra years of life and vastly improved health decades later, in old age" (Kolata 2007). Dr. Lleras-Muney, an economist at Princeton University who has examined educational policies in different countries and their influence on health and longevity, notes that "In every country, compelling children to spend a longer time in school led to better health" (quoted in Kolata 2007). Why education is correlated with better health and longevity is disputed. Kolata mentions a hypothesis that posits a link between education, planning for the future, and the renunciation of immediate pleasure:

> Dr. Lleras-Muney and others point to one plausible explanation — as a group, less educated people are less able to plan for the future and to delay gratification. . . . [E]ducation, Dr. Smith at Rand finds, may somehow teach people to delay gratification. . . . "Most of adherence is unpleasant," Dr. Smith says. "You have to be willing to do something that is not pleasant now and you have to stay with it and think about the future." . . . He deplores the dictums to live in the moment or to live for today. That advice, Dr. Smith says, is "the worst thing for your health." (Kolata 2007)

This advice may or may not be convincing, and few schools are likely to promote the idea that they will help you live longer because they are unpleasant. Nonetheless, in assuming that people can live long lives and plan for their futures, the author and the authorities cited can hardly be accused of presupposing a bizarre, highly artificial concept of persons.

In the second article, "Free Will: Now You Have It, Now You Don't," Dennis Overbye reflects on our ordinary belief that we are free to make choices that lead to plans for the future by drawing our attention to the practice of making New Year resolutions. "Having just lived through another New Year's Eve, many of you have just resolved to be better, wiser, stronger and richer in the coming months and years. After all, we're free humans, not slaves, robots or animals doomed to repeat the same boring mistakes over and over again. As William James wrote, the whole 'sting and excitement' of life comes from 'our sense that in it things are really being decided from one moment to another.' . . . I could skip the chocolate cake, I really could, but why bother? Waiter!" (Overbye 2007).

The two stories are at odds: one counsels us to endure the unpleasant aspect of education to live longer, while the other counsels immediate satisfaction in spontaneous freedom. Still, it is instructive to see that both articles rest on what may be called a natural or commonsense picture of ourselves. That picture (which Churchland calls the folk psychological concept of ourselves) includes the recognition of thoughts, beliefs, perceptions, desires, and performances. It also, in philosophical terms, includes recognition of the following: Each of us is a substantial self, an individual or person, who is capable of persisting as the same self through or across time. The self that exists at a later time is identical with the self that exists at earlier times. While a self might change by becoming more educated, the more-educated self is the same self as that which was less educated. This may seem mind-numbingly obvious, but we shall see in chapter 1 how some forms of naturalism challenge this ordinary self-understanding.

Additional assumptions in the articles are as follows: Because a self is a substantial individual, it has various properties. Most importantly, the self has the capacity to experience pleasure and the different capacity to experience pain. A self also has the power to conceive of or imagine its future and that future being better or worse. In light of the capacity to conceive of its future, a self purposely makes choices about and plans how to act in the future. These choices at least appear to be undetermined by the forces or powers around us. That is, in ordinary experience, it seems that it is in some deep sense up to you whether or not you will choose to skip the chocolate cake. A self that makes such choices for purposes or reasons is said to have "libertarian free will." The making of good choices and plans is wise or rational. The making of bad choices and plans is unwise or irrational. The making of choices, good or bad, is explained by purposes or goals, and the actions chosen are performed to bring into reality the purpose or goal that explains the choice to perform them. Philosophers often say such purposive explanations are *teleological* (after *telos*, the Greek term for "purpose") in nature.

Though much more could be said about what we are describing as the natural view of ourselves, for our purposes one more datum is particularly relevant. In an article entitled "Black Freshmen Are More Religious Than Their Peers, Survey Finds" in the *Chronicle of Higher Education*, Thomas Bartlett points out that most American college students are quite religious. According to a survey titled "Spirituality in Higher Education: A National Study of College Students' Search for Meaning and Purpose," "95 per cent of African-American students believe in God, compared with 84 percent of Latino, 78 percent of white, and 65 percent of Asian-American students" (Bartlett 2005). The religious nature of college professors, though not as high as that of students, is higher than one might think. In "Professors Are More Religious Than Some Might Assume, Survey Finds," also in the *Chronicle of Higher Education*, Bartlett reports that "Nearly one-fifth of respondents said they believed in a 'higher power of some kind.' An additional 36 percent said they had no doubts about the existence of God, while 17 percent generally believed in God but had some doubts" (Bartlett 2006).

We do not assume from these and other studies that religious belief today is as natural as believing that persons persist over time, have experiences of pleasure and pain, and make good or bad choices. Rather, we simply point out that religious conceptions of ourselves are not at all uncommon and are even widespread in secular educational institutions. Therefore, our project in this book will be not just to examine the implications of naturalism for an ostensible "commonsense" view of ourselves, but also to consider the bearing of naturalism on a religious conception of reality.

Nature and Naturalism: Some Preliminary Distinctions

In the previous section we sketched what we believe is a natural portrait of ourselves. But what does it mean for something to be natural? That which is natural is presumably that which accords with nature. But what is nature?

In ancient Greek and Roman philosophy, the natural world was often conceived of as purposive and laden with values. For Aristotle, for example, the nature of a plant was its power to grow, and possibly its power to nourish or heal. In this framework harm and evil consisted of damage to something's nature. So the evil of a child wantonly killing a parent or a tyrant engaged in capricious violence was a violation of the very nature of a family or the nature of a political community. Many Christian medievalists embraced a similar philosophy of nature. Saint Thomas Aquinas, for example, held that nature is fundamentally good, that evil is a destruction of good nature, and that divine grace perfects nature. Redemption of nature was seen as the *consummation* of nature, not its *violation* or *annihilation.*

With the development of modern science, this value-laden understanding of nature was challenged by a more mechanical, value-neutral portrait. As nature came to be primarily described and explained in terms of mathematics and geometry, intense philosophical work concentrated on how human beings are related to nature. Gradually this modern, scientifically oriented philosophy of nature eroded the ideal that the nature of a human being is a stable, moral reference point. Thomas Hobbes (seventeenth century) argued that human thought and consciousness were matter in motion. Baron d'Holbach (eighteenth century) conjectured that we are machines. Baruch Spinoza (seventeenth century) celebrated "nature" as central to his philosophy — his key principle was *natura naturans,* or "nature naturing" — with human beings, like all reality, subject to and completely determined by exceptionless, impersonal laws. David Hume (eighteenth century) proposed that the natural world cares nothing for human beings, and John Stuart Mill (nineteenth century) more aggressively compared "Nature" to a sociopathic murderer, a force that cruelly destroys its members without conscience, purpose, or consciousness.

Naturalism — very roughly — may be defined as the philosophy that *everything that exists is a part of nature and that there is no reality beyond or outside of nature*. While this is a serviceable overall definition, it is clearly not very informative or precise. If "nature" is understood in the older, broader sense in which everything that has a nature is natural, then God, angels, and departed souls may be classified as natural (theologians have speculated about the nature of God, angels, and the soul). The really interesting philosophical debates arise when it comes to specifying what might be called *the nature of nature*, identifying what is being positively affirmed as part of nature or what is natural and what is definitively excluded. Is "nature" to be understood along the lines of Hobbes, d'Holbach, Spinoza, Hume, and Mill? Or should "nature" be conceived of as including not only matter in motion but also souls, freedom of the will, and purposes that explain actions? Is there any way for naturalism to accommodate the notion that nature is fundamentally good?

The vagueness of the terms "naturalism" and "nature" generates some frustration these days. We are in an intellectual climate in which there is a near consensus that naturalism is the philosophically correct dominant framework for nearly all areas of philosophical inquiry, but also no consensus over precisely what is meant by "naturalism" and "nature." Echoing Nagel's complaint about the "notorious" lack of specificity in defining naturalism, Barry Stroud writes:

> "Naturalism" seems to me ... rather like "World Peace." Almost everyone swears allegiance to it, and is willing to march under its banner. But disputes can still break out about what it is appropriate or acceptable to do in the name of that slogan. And like world peace, once you start specifying concretely exactly what it involves and how to achieve it, it becomes increasingly difficult to reach and to sustain a consistent and exclusive "naturalism." There is pressure on the one hand to include more and more within your conception of "nature," so it loses its definiteness and restrictiveness. Or, if the conception is kept fixed and restrictive, there is pressure on the other hand to distort or even to deny the very phenomena that a naturalistic study — and especially a naturalistic study of human beings — is supposed to explain. (Stroud 2004, 22)

Worry about the vagueness of the term "naturalism" is well documented. In 1922 Roy Wood Sellars claimed, "We are naturalists now. But, even so, this common naturalism is of a very vague and general sort, capable of covering an immense diversity of opinion. It is an admission of a direction more than a clearly formulated belief" (Sellars 1922, vii).

Our goal in this short book is to display the promise and perils of contemporary naturalism, taking into account different, competing definitions of naturalism and the natural world. Chapter 1 begins with a strict definition of naturalism. According to what may be called "strict naturalism," nature is all that exists and nature itself is whatever will be disclosed by the ideal natural sciences, especially physics. The reason for appealing to the "ideal" natural sciences is that today our sciences are still incomplete — there are abundant events not yet precisely described, let alone explained. For a scientific, strict naturalist, the best guide to reality is the ideal (ever elusive) *complete* natural scientific worldview. We argue in chapter 2 that this form of naturalism faces insurmountable problems, especially in accounting for the most salient features of what we described in the previous section as the natural view of ourselves. We think strict naturalism cannot successfully describe, accommodate, or undermine either the reality of purposeful explanation, or libertarian free choices, or experiences of pleasure and pain, or the existence of persons.

In chapter 3 our assessment of strict naturalism takes shape in the context of assessing the naturalist critique of what ordinary people and philosophers like Plato and Descartes refer to as the soul. Virtually all forms of naturalism, but especially the strict variety, reject what is known as soul-body or mind-body dualism (dualism, for short), the view that persons are or include something nonphysical. Dualism is the view that manifests itself in the ordinary belief that persons are substantial, individual beings who persist self-identical through time. It is our souls that endure across time, notwithstanding the radical changes in our bodies (e.g., most or all of the components of our physical bodies are changed over the course of about seven years). The deep-seated nature of dualism is evidenced in a great deal of classical and religious literature. For one of the more recent examples of dualism in present-day culture, consider the hugely popular Harry Potter novels, where the worst death one can die is to have one's soul sucked out of one's body by the kiss of a being called a dementor. And the contemporary antidualist philosopher John Searle reports that "[w]hen I lectured on the mind-body problem in India [I] was assured by several members of my audience that my views must be mistaken, because they personally had existed in their earlier lives as frogs or elephants, etc." (Searle 1992, 91). The cogency of naturalism can be measured to the extent that it can show this nonnaturalist dualist view of people to be mistaken.

Assessing *strict naturalism,* however, is far from fully addressing the powerful movement of naturalism. As Sellars rightly observes: "To define naturalism in a narrow and indefensible way and then to tear it to pieces may be a pleasant enough dialectical exercise but surely it is not consonant with the serious aim of philosophy to discover the truth about nature and ourselves as children of nature" (Sellars 1922, vii). In chapter 4 we address broader conceptions of naturalism that recognize that we "children of nature" have conscious, subjective experiences, and we live in a world of great value. These more expansive versions of naturalism are given various titles in the current literature, such as "liberal naturalism," "more open-minded or expansive naturalism," "nonscientific naturalism," and "pluralistic naturalism" as opposed to "restrictive" or "puritanical" or simply "scientific" naturalism. (For a sampling of these terms, see De Caro and Macarthur 2004.) We will simply use the term "broad naturalism" to name these more expanded conceptions of the natural world.

The crucial element uniting most of these broader forms of naturalism is that they reject the view that there is anything in the world that cannot (ultimately) be accounted for in terms of the sciences, *including* psychology, history, and so on. Broad naturalists allow for more than physics, chemistry, and biology, but they retain a stern resistance to appeals to any force beyond the natural world such as a transcendent God to account for the existence and character of nature. It is especially this last point — the rejection of theism — that unites naturalists of whatever sort, strict or broad. Stroud correctly underscores the antitheistic or what he describes as antisupernaturalist meaning of naturalism.

In the sense in which naturalism is opposed to supernaturalism there has been no recent naturalistic turn in philosophy. Most philosophers for at least one hundred years have been naturalists in the nonsupernaturalist sense. They have taken it for granted that any satisfactory account of how human belief and knowledge in general are possible will involve only processes and events of the intelligible natural world, without the intervention or reassurance of any supernatural agent. Many people regard that as, on the whole, a good thing. But it is nothing new. (Stroud 2004, 23)

The following antitheistic definition of naturalism advocated by Kai Nielsen is also representative of the attitude of naturalists in the current, philosophical literature: "Naturalism denies that there are any spiritual or supernatural realities. There are, that is, no purely mental substances and there are no supernatural realities transcendent to the world or at least we have no good ground for believing that there could be such realities. . . . It is the view that anything that exists is ultimately composed of physical components" (Nielsen 1997, 402; see also Nielsen 1996). In chapter 4 we consider this primarily antisupernatural form of broad naturalism and its challenge in accounting for consciousness and values.

Chapter 5 seeks to challenge more directly the almost unquestioned primacy of naturalism. Searle (himself a naturalist) has described the current intellectual climate of dogmatically assuming a materialistic naturalism in a fashion that approximates religion (which, for Searle, is not good). "There is a sense in which materialism is the religion of our time, at least among most of the professional experts in the fields of philosophy, psychology, cognitive science, and other disciplines that study the mind. Like more traditional religions, it is accepted without question and it provides the framework within which other questions can be posed, addressed and answered" (Searle 2004, 48). The dogmatism of naturalism has however been assailed. Over the last thirty years there have been serious challenges to the naturalistic framework in both its strict and broad formats and a dynamic revival of philosophical theism. Chapter 5 takes up the question whether the naturalistic rejection of theism — the central common bond between strict and broad naturalism — is vindicated.

The attention we give to theism may lead some readers to think the book should be retitled *Naturalism and Theism*. While the suggestion has merit, we resist this for three reasons. First, our central concern is indeed naturalism, while theism comes into focus principally because there is a central, overriding consensus among contemporary naturalists that theism is false or incoherent. In fact, as Stroud has observed, being antitheistic is the one point virtually all naturalists can agree on.

Second, contemporary naturalists have been increasingly regarding theism as a key testing ground for naturalism. Stroud suggests that the demise of theism is taken for granted by many contemporary naturalists. But that this is not always so may be observed in the publication of Daniel Dennett's *Breaking the Spell: Religion as a Natural Phenomenon* (2006). Dennett is clear about the importance of assessing religion from a naturalist point of view. Religion "affects not just our social, political, and economic conflicts, but the very meaning we find in our lives. For many people, probably a majority of the people on Earth, nothing matters more than religion" (Dennett 2006, 14-15). Dennett, like the naturalist Hume before him, fully recognizes the importance of countering a nonnaturalist, theistic worldview. Hence, a book on naturalism needs to consider whether, for example, the following dismissal of theism by Bertrand Russell on naturalistic grounds is vindicated.

> God and immortality, the central dogmas of the Christian religion, find no support in science. . . . No doubt people will continue to entertain these beliefs, because they are pleasant, just as it is pleasant to think ourselves virtuous and our enemies wicked. But for my part I cannot see any ground for either. I do not pretend to be able to prove that there is no God. I equally cannot prove that Satan is a fiction. The Christian God may exist; so may the Gods of Olympus, or of ancient Egypt, or of Babylon. But no one of these hypotheses is more probable than any other; *they lie outside the region of even probable knowledge, and therefore there is no reason to consider any of them.* (Russell 1957, 44, emphasis added)

This passage brings up a third reason why a book on naturalism needs to take theism seriously. Naturalists today often work with a scientific understanding of what counts as a good explanation, according to which if there is a God, then the existence of God would have to be assessed as a scientific hypothesis. This is evidently the position of one of the more outspoken critics of religion today, the naturalist Richard Dawkins. He writes: "I pay religions the compliment of regarding them as scientific theories and . . . I see God as a competing explanation for facts about the universe and life. This is certainly how God has been seen by most theologians of past centuries and by most ordinary religious people today. . . . Either admit that God is a scientific hypothesis and let him submit to the same judgment as any other scientific hypothesis. Or admit that his status is no higher than that of fairies and river sprites" (Dawkins 1995, 46-47). At the heart of Dawkins's form of naturalism is the claim that an all-encompassing scientific stance on the world is vastly superior to any competitor such as religion. This scientific philosophy is shared by E. O. Wilson in his critique of religion. "The reasons why I consider the scientific ethos superior to religion [are]: its repeated triumphs in explaining and controlling the physical world; its self-correcting nature open to all competent [people] to devise and conduct the tests; its readiness to examine all subjects sacred and profane; and now the possibility of explaining traditional religion by the mechanistic models of evolutionary biology" (Wilson 1978, 201). This book explores the strengths and possible weaknesses of Dawkins's and Wilson's concept of the scientific method, raising the question whether the existence or nonexistence of God is best thought of as a scientific or, more broadly, a philosophical matter.

In the end, the problem that afflicts Russell's, Dawkins's, Dennett's, and Wilson's naturalistic critique of religion, theism, and the existence of God is that each supposes that the sciences can replace or weaken the appeal to God as the transcendent reality that conserves the existence of the cosmos or what they call "nature." We hope to show in subsequent chapters that a sound philosophical inquiry into the nature of contemporary versions of naturalism will reveal that there is absolutely nothing antiscientific about what we are describing as a natural understanding of ourselves. One can embrace both that understanding and the different sciences (e.g., physics, biology, and chemistry) without embracing naturalism in any of its contemporary incarnations. Indeed, we believe the explanatory successes of the different sciences raise the broader question about why there is a cosmos in which these successes are achieved, and this, in turn, raises questions about what transcends the cosmos.

CHAPTER I

The Challenge of Strict Naturalism

I had a dream, and I heard in my dream that the primeval letters of elements out of which you and I and all other things are compounded have no reason or explanation.

Plato, *Theaetetus*

In the introduction we cited Sellars's claim that "we are all naturalists now." Even if this were true, it is doubtful that we would all be the same kind of naturalist. In this chapter we describe a form of naturalism that not all self-described naturalists accept. We begin with what may be called "strict naturalism" both because it elicits widespread support in the philosophical and scientific communities and because of its radical implications about nature and human nature. In strict naturalism the natural beliefs about ourselves described in the introduction are, in the end, false; our "natural beliefs" may be accorded some pragmatic utility, but they do not accurately describe fundamental features of human nature. If strict naturalism is true, then there is no ultimate and irreducible teleological explanation of any event, let alone our actions, in terms of a purpose; there is no libertarian freedom of the will; there are no irreducible experiences of pleasure and pain; there is no enduring self or soul of any kind; and God, if God exists, is explanatorily irrelevant to events that occur in our world.

Though there is no universally agreed-upon definition of strict naturalism, it is possible to cobble together a fairly clear characterization of it, even if this characterization is to some extent an idealization. Strict naturalism typically begins with a statement to the effect that all that exists is a part of nature and something is a part of nature if and only if it is describable and explainable in an ideal, complete science or, more specifically, physics. Jerry Fodor describes his own scientifically focused form of strict naturalism as a kind of "scientism":

> I hold to a philosophical view that, for want of a better term, I'll call by one that is usually taken to be pejorative: *Scientism.* Scientism claims, on the one hand, that the goals of scientific inquiry include the discovery of objective empirical truths; and on the other hand, that science has come pretty close to achieving this goal at least from time to time. The molecular theory of gasses, I suppose, is a plausible example of achieving it in physics; so is cell theory in biology; the theory, in geology, that the earth is very old; and the theory, in astronomy, that the stars are very far away. . . . I'm inclined to think that Scientism, so construed, is not just true but *obviously and certainly* true; it's something that nobody in the late twentieth century who has a claim to an adequate education and a minimum of common sense should doubt. (Fodor 2002, 30, emphasis Fodor's)

This is a fairly modest statement, and few will disagree with it. But strict naturalists go further: Given the overwhelming accomplishment of the sciences, why not assume that an ideal science will give us an ideal account of *all* reality? The prestigious *Encyclopedia of Philosophy* entry for "naturalism" forcefully describes naturalists as "repudiating the view that there exists *or could exist* any entities or events which lie, in principle, beyond the scope of scientific explanation" (Danto 1967, 448, emphasis added). On this view, even the possibility of something transcending science is ruled out. While some naturalists uphold the natural sciences in general (physics, chemistry, biology), some give physics a privileged place. For example, David Papineau believes that strict naturalism is a commitment to the completeness of physics, where physics is complete in the sense that a purely physical specification of the world, plus physical laws, will always suffice to explain what happens (Papineau 1993). He is aware that the concepts of physics change over time. What categories, therefore, will qualify as "physical" in the ultimate or final physics? We cannot, says Papineau, presently answer this question with any certitude. At best we can specify one category that will not qualify for inclusion, namely, the category of the psychological attitudes such as beliefs, desires, and choices that represent things as being a certain way:

> When I say that a complete physics excludes psychology, and that psychological antecedents are therefore never needed to explain physical effects, the emphasis here is on "needed." I am quite happy to allow that psychological categories *can* be used to explain physical effects, as when I tell you that my arm rose because I wanted to lift it. My claim is only that in all such cases an alternative specification of a sufficient antecedent, which does not mention psychological categories, will also be available. (Papineau 1993, 31 n. 26, emphasis Papineau's)

On this view, psychological accounts of events are superseded by sufficient, nonpsychological accounts; in other words, a sufficient explanation of your bodily movements can be given with no reference to your intentions, desires, and feelings. Consider one other characterization of physics and what it excludes: "We may not know enough about physics to know exactly what a complete 'physics' might include. But as long as we are confident that, whatever it includes, it will have no ineliminable need for any distinctively mental categorizations, we can be confident that mental properties must be identical with (or realized by) certain non-mentally identifiable properties" (Papineau 2002, 41).

David Armstrong is another philosopher who advocates strict naturalism by proposing that ideal physics has an ultimately privileged explanatory role. According to Armstrong, strict naturalism is "the doctrine that reality consists of nothing but a single all-embracing spatio-temporal system" (Armstrong 1978, 261). Contemporary physicalism or materialism (the view that everything that exists is physical or material in nature) is a form of strict naturalism and maintains that the single, all-embracing temporal system contains nothing but the entities recognized by the most mature physics. Irreducible purpose or teleology has no place in this (or any other) spatiotemporal system as an ultimate or basic explanatory principle because it entails the characteristic of irreducible intention-

15

ality, and intentionality implies the falsity of strict naturalism. Thus, Armstrong says that "if the principles involved [in analyzing the single, all-embracing spatiotemporal system that is reality] were completely different from the current principles of physics, in particular if they involved appeal to mental entities, such as purposes, we might then count the analysis as a falsification of Naturalism" (262).

The goal of strict naturalism is to take the beliefs, desires, preferences, choices, and so on that appear to make up our conscious, intelligent, psychological life and explain them in terms that are nonconscious, nonmental, and nonpsychological. Georges Rey insists that any proper explanation of the mental must be in terms that are nonmental. Otherwise, there will be no explanation. "Any ultimate explanation of mental phenomena will have to be in *non*-mental terms, or else it won't be an *explanation* of it. There might be an explanation of some mental phenomena in terms of others — perhaps *hope* in terms of *belief* and *desire* — but if we are to provide an explanation of all mental phenomena, we would in turn have to explain such mentalistic explainers until finally we reached entirely non-mental terms" (Rey 1997, 21, emphasis Rey's). Dennett agrees. "Only a theory that explained conscious events in terms of unconscious events could explain consciousness at all" (Dennett 1991, 454).

Strict naturalism, as an ideal scientific philosophy, seeks to include all aspects of reality within a comprehensive and unified perspective that excludes anything that is either conscious, or psychological, or mental in nature. Thus, not only does it ultimately exclude any teleological explanatory role for purposes with the result that no explanation can ultimately include mention of them (in this sense, strict naturalism countenances only purposeless explanations), but it also excludes or is incompatible with the view that agents make undetermined, free choices. Strict naturalism is incompatible with libertarian freedom because undetermined free choices are choices that are ultimately explained by the purposes of the agents who make them. Hence, because strict naturalism excludes ultimate teleological explanations in terms of purposes, it excludes libertarian free will.

While strict naturalists are advocates of scientism, they nevertheless recognize that we ordinarily think of ourselves as having libertarian freedom. Thinking that we have such freedom may be part of the folk psychology that we employ in everyday events, but when we turn to the philosophy and science of action, such psychology is, in Churchland's phrase, "probably mistaken." In other words, when strict naturalists do talk about human actions, they insist that all action is determined to occur by nonmental events. Francis Crick (the codiscoverer of the molecular structure of DNA) is quite clear about this. While he acknowledges that we have an "undeniable feeling that our Will is free," he also maintains "that our Will only appears to be free" (Crick 1994, 10). In whatever sense it is true to say that we choose, Crick believes that a choice is completely determined to occur. Dennett agrees with Crick. According to Dennett, any kind of freedom that we have must be a kind that is compatible with the truth of determinism (Dennett 1984, 2003). While he concedes that we are not aware of the causes of our choices, this ignorance can be explained:

> Whatever else we are, we are information-processing systems, and all information-processing systems rely on amplifiers of a sort. Relatively small causes are made to yield relatively large effects. . . . Vast amounts of information arrive on the coattails of negligible amounts of energy, and then, thanks to amplification powers of systems of switches, the information begins to do some work, . . . leading eventually to an action whose pedigree of efficient . . . causation is so hopelessly inscrutable as to be invisible. We see the dramatic effects leaving; we don't see the causes entering; we are tempted by the hypothesis that there are no causes. (Dennett 1984, 76-77)

In short, from our failure to be aware of causes of our choices we cannot reasonably conclude that there are none. This is because the causes are beyond our ken. Therefore, our lack of awareness of them is to be expected and in no way supports or justifies a belief in their absence, just as the failure to be aware of a needle on the floor of a field house with bleachers in no way justifies belief that no needle is on that floor. Owen Flanagan summarizes this point nicely:

> [T]he myth of a completely self-initiating ego, an unmoved but self-moving will, [is] simply a fiction motivated by our ignorance of the causes of human behavior. [There is] no need for the notion of a meta-

17

physically unconstrained will or of an independent ego as an unconstrained primal cause in order to have a robust conception of free
agency. For there to be agency we need the ego as a cause, possibly
even the proximate cause of what we do. But the ego may serve as the
proximate cause of action and still itself be part of the causal nexus.
(Flanagan 2002, 112)

Given that strict naturalism maintains that all explanation is
nonpurposive in nature and that the human self or ego and its activity
are part of a deterministic causal nexus, it is not surprising that strict
naturalism also claims that there is no radical bifurcation between a person or self and its physical body. In other words, strict naturalism holds
that dualism, the view that persons are or possess an immaterial mind or
soul, is false. There couldn't be this kind of duality, given that the ideal
physics cannot recognize the reality of anything that is psychological or
mental in nature. Thus, while scientific, strict naturalism acknowledges
the apparent duality between the mental self with its subjective experiences and purposes and the physical world that includes its (the self's)
body, it maintains that this duality is ultimately illusory.

This rejection of dualism is fundamental to strict naturalism as well
as virtually all forms of naturalism. Consider Flanagan's advocacy of
what he sees as the powerful scientific image of persons. "There is no
consensus yet about the details of the scientific image of persons. But
there is broad agreement about how we must construct this detailed picture. First, we will need to demythologize persons by rooting out certain
unfounded ideas from the perennial philosophy. Letting go of the belief
in souls is a minimal requirement. In fact, desouling is the primary operation of the scientific image" (Flanagan 2002, 3).

Sometimes the rejection of dualism is couched in terms of the rejection of an enduring, substantial self that remains self-identical through
time. For example, Dennett advocates a strict form of naturalism that
entails that we, qua minds, are not substantial selves but systems of organized parts.

We now understand that the mind is not, as Descartes confusedly supposed, in *communication with* the brain in some miraculous way; it *is*

the brain, or, more specifically, a system or organization within the brain that has evolved in much the way that our immune system or respiratory system or digestive system has evolved. Like many other natural wonders, the human mind is something of a bag of tricks, cobbled together over the eons by the foresightless process of evolution by natural selection. (Dennett 2006, 107, emphasis Dennett's)

In an interview on the same subject, Dennett maintains that the idea of a substantial self, which is the self that we experience from the first-person point of view, must ultimately be accounted for in terms that do not admit its existence. In other words, the substantial self cannot form part of the final theory of what exists. "You've got to leave the first person [substantial self] out of your final theory. You won't have a theory of consciousness if you still have the first person in there, because that was what it was your job to explain. All the paraphernalia that doesn't make any sense unless you've got a first person in there, has to be turned into something else. You've got to figure out some way to break it up and distribute its powers and opportunities into the system in some other way" (Dennett in Blackmore 2006, 87).

In the same interview Dennett is asked how he addresses what seems to be the recurrent intuition or apparent experience that the self is the substantial subject of experiences. The interviewer queries: "I can get quite upset about — say — the brownness of this desk here; the 'how it seems to me.' I have the powerful experience that I [a substantial self] am in here [the self's body] experiencing this ineffable [not describable in more basic terms], unique, private sensation of the brownness, can you help me?" Dennett replies:

The way I recommend is to ask yourself, "What am I pointing to? What am I ostending when I say *this?*" What I think you'll find is that you can start elaborating a sort of catalogue of the facts that matter to you at this moment. Maybe it's the particular deliciousness of this taste in my mouth; so what is that deliciousness? Well, I'd like some more, and I can recall it at a later date, and so on. We're going to take care of all that. We're going to include your disposition to want some more, your capacity to recollect, and even the likelihood that you will find yourself pleasurably recollecting this experience of it. There's a huge manifold of reactive dispositions that you're pointing to when you're saying, "This very yumminess right now," and what you have to do is recognize that however indissolvable, however unassailable, however intrinsically present that all seems to you, what has to be explained is that it seems to you, not that it is so. (Blackmore 2006, 88, emphasis Dennett's)

On this view, our states of experience and ostensible experience of ourselves need to be explained away.

Now it is possible to draw a distinction between a self that has a psychological or mental life and that mental life. Hence, one might think that it is possible to eliminate the existence of the soul while holding on to the reality of psychological properties (e.g., the capacity to believe and the capacity to experience pain) and corresponding events (e.g., believing that it is raining today and experiencing pain in one's foot). In other words, one might think that while there are no souls but only physical entities, some of those physical entities (e.g., human beings) have two kinds of properties, namely, physical and psychological, and their corresponding events. What needs to be understood is that strict naturalism denies even this less robust kind of dualism. (What we will call "broad naturalism" tries to accommodate the data of this weaker form of dualism, and we will take this up in later chapters.)

One way to clarify the idea of the complete elimination of the psychological is in terms of contemporary brain-imaging techniques and the distinction between the first- and third-person points of view. For example, a neurological examination of your brain states will reveal neurons firing but will not make directly observable the feelings (e.g., anxiety) that the neurological events are causing. It seems that you can know you are anxious from a first-person, privileged access, but science is, as it were, third person in nature. In *Naturalizing the Mind,* Fred Dretske contends that this apparent duality of perspectives can be overcome to usher in a scientifically unified understanding of persons and nature.

For a materialist there are no facts that are accessible to only one person. . . . If the subjective life of another being, what it is like to be a creature, seems inaccessible, this must be because we fail to understand what we are talking about when we talk about its subjective states. If S feels some way, and its feeling some way is a material state, how can it be impossible for us to know how S feels? . . . Though each of us has direct information about our own experience, there is no privileged access. If you know where to look, you can get the same information I have about the character of my experiences. This is a result of thinking about the mind in naturalistic terms. Subjectivity becomes part of the objective order. For materialists, this is how it should be. (Dretske 1995, 65)

The idea that subjective experience may be either eliminated or fully incorporated in an exclusively scientific understanding of the world is espoused by virtually every strict naturalist.

Churchland insists that to claim that there is more to human persons than what will be disclosed in the physical sciences is akin to vitalism, the discredited thesis that "life" is a kind of explanatory force that cannot be accounted for in terms of the dynamics and organization of lifeless (dead) molecules. But, "however closely you might watch these molecular structures folding, unfolding, hooking, and drifting aimlessly around in the soup, it is obvious that you would never observe the impulse of life that urges its growth; you would never observe the telos of life that knows and guides its species-specific development" (Churchland 1995, 192). Just as vitalism has given way to a less mystical life science, the neuroscience of today has no need to leave room for the explanation of certain events in terms of nonphysical causes and purposes.

The unified incorporation of all phenomena in a naturalistic scientific philosophy means that the difference between being a fully conscious human being (or some other animal) and any inanimate matter and energy is chiefly a matter of complexity, configuration, and function rather than of nature or substance. Here are two bold, unapologetic statements of this complexity thesis of strict naturalism by two well-known writers about science, Carl Sagan (a cosmologist) and Crick:

I am a collection of water, calcium, and organic molecules called Carl Sagan. You are a collection of almost identical molecules with a different collective label. But is that all? Is there nothing in here but molecules? Some people find this idea somehow demeaning to human dignity. For myself, I find it elevating that our universe permits the evolution of molecular machines as intricate and subtle as we. But the essence of life is not so much the atoms and simple molecules that make us up as the way in which they are put together. (Sagan 1980, 105)

The Astonishing Hypothesis is that "You," your joys and your sorrows, your memories and your ambitions, your sense of identity and free will, are in fact no more than the behavior of a vast assembly of nerve cells and their associated molecules. As Lewis Carroll's Alice may have phrased it: "You're nothing but a pack of neurons." This hypothesis is so alien to the ideas of most people alive today that it can be truly called astonishing. (Crick 1994, 3)

The comments of Sagan and Crick might suggest that scientific, strict naturalism is compatible with recognizing Sagan's and Crick's reality as selves with feelings (e.g., Sagan's elation), but this would be a mistake. Susan Blackmore, who adopts Dennett's account of the self, writes: "I long ago concluded that there is no substantial or persistent self to be found in experience, let alone in the brain. I have become quite uncertain as to whether there really is anything it is like to be me" (Blackmore 2006, 9). The radical consequences of strict naturalism are also expressed quite clearly by Richard Rorty. He makes clear that a final, complete philosophy should eliminate any ultimate appeal to feelings and other mental states. Rorty even thinks the reality of pain as a feeling may well be rejected. "The absurdity of saying 'Nobody has ever felt a pain' is no greater than that of saying 'Nobody has ever seen a demon,' if we have a suitable answer to the question 'What was I reporting when I said I felt pain?' To this question, the science of the future may reply 'You were reporting the occurrence of a certain brain process, and it would make life simpler for us if you would, in the future, say "My C-fibers are firing," instead of saying "I'm in pain"'" (Rorty 1965, 30).

Because the implications of strict naturalism for things such as teleological explanation, libertarian free will, the soul, and our mental lives are, dare we say, hard to *believe*, a strict naturalist such as Dennett sometimes claims that he is not denying the everyday sense in which we think of ourselves as conscious, enduring subjects; he is simply explaining what it is to be a conscious self, rather than explaining it away. But at the same time, he insists that the "final theory" of what exists and why it exists must not contain any appeal to causally efficacious selves who act for purposes. The true spirit of Dennett's view is nicely expressed in his lampooning of David Chalmers. In response to Chalmers's claim that the reality of experience is a datum that must be acknowledged, Dennett says experience is like cuteness:

> We can see this by comparing Chalmers' proposal with yet one more imaginary non-starter: *cutism*, the proposal that since some things are just plain cute, and other things aren't cute at all — you can just see it, however hard it is to describe or explain — we had better postulate *cuteness* as a fundamental property of physics alongside mass, charge and space-time. (Cuteness is *not* a functional property, of course; I can imagine somebody who wasn't actually cute at all but who nevertheless functioned exactly as if cute — trust me.) Cutism is in even worse shape than vitalism. Nobody would have taken vitalism seriously for a minute if the vitalists hadn't had a set of independently describable phenomena — of reproduction, metabolism, self-repair and the like — that their postulated fundamental life-element was hoped to account for. Once these phenomena were otherwise accounted for, vitalism fell flat, but at least it had a project. Until Chalmers gives an independent ground for contemplating the drastic move of adding "experience" to mass, charge, and space-time, his proposal is one that can be put on the back burner. (Dennett 2000, 35, emphasis Dennett's)

On Dennett's view, there is no reason to give presumptive weight to the seemingly irreducible nature of certain features of the world and our thought about and experience of it. After all, as a reductive explanation of certain commonsense features of physical objects (e.g., color, sound, taste, and smell), the atomic theory of matter may seem initially quite counterintuitive, but it has proven to be quite successful (though we doubt that it has successfully reduced color, sound, taste, and smell to

23

atomic particles in motion). Though it may initially seem equally counterintuitive that the atomic theory of matter can provide an adequate reductive explanation of our thought and experience, there is no good reason to doubt that it will be equally successful in this domain as well.

In conclusion, it is obvious that strict naturalism has radical implications for various aspects of the natural view of ourselves such as purposeful explanation, libertarian freedom, the soul, and what we experience. In the next chapter we consider in detail some powerful arguments for and against strict naturalism.

CHAPTER 2

Strict Naturalism versus a Natural View of Persons

[Certain people] have an instinctive horror of any "explaining away" of the soul. I don't know why certain people have this horror while others, like me, find in reductionism the ultimate religion. Perhaps my lifelong training in physics and science in general has given me a deep awe at seeing how the most substantial and familiar objects of experience fade away, as one approaches the infinitesimal scale, into an eerily insubstantial ether, a myriad of ephemeral swirling vortices of nearly incomprehensible mathematical activity.

Douglas Hofstadter, "Reductionism and Religion"

Strict naturalism contests the truth of the natural understanding of ourselves. It maintains that there are no ultimate and irreducible purposeful explanations of events, that there is no libertarian free will, and that there are no irreducible psychological or mental properties and events. While in chapter 4 we will consider broader concepts of naturalism that countenance retaining some of these elements of the natural view of ourselves, strict naturalism is more severe. As the strict naturalist Churchland writes: "Is our basic conception of human cognition and agency yet another myth, moderately useful in the past perhaps, yet false at its edge or core? Will a proper theory of brain function present a significantly different or incompatible portrait of human nature? . . . I am inclined toward positive answers to all these questions" (Churchland

1995, 19). In this chapter we look more closely at some of the reasons behind strict naturalism and some of the challenges it faces.

Given the assault of strict naturalism on the very core of our natural view of ourselves, what is one to say about it? One argument against strict naturalism would be to maintain that the view is self-defeating: its proponents *believe* that it is true and seek to convince us of its truth, whereas if the view is true, then there ultimately is no such thing as *believing that it is true* because *there ultimately are no psychological events of any kind, period.* While we are convinced that this is a perfectly legitimate argument to make in response to strict naturalism, we simply note it here in passing. (For a cogent argument that strict naturalism is self-refuting, see Hasker 1999.) Our concern in this chapter can be formed as a question: Why would anyone think that strict naturalism is true? We pointed out in chapter 1 that the explanatory successes of science have led some to believe that everything can be explained in nonteleological, physical causal terms. A study of the literature about strict naturalism, however, leads one to believe that in the end strict naturalists appeal to one central argument in support of their view — "the argument from causal closure." Philosopher of science Karl Popper's comment about physicalism is apropos for naturalism as well: "the physicalist principle of the closedness of the physical [world] . . . is of decisive importance, and I take it as the characteristic principle of physicalism or materialism" (Popper and Eccles 1977, 51).

In the next section we discuss further the natural view of ourselves. We then examine the credibility of the argument from the causal closure of the physical world and go on to consider whether it is plausible to hold that our apparent experiences and mental states are indeed mythic or merely folk beliefs that should be displaced by the physical sciences.

Strict Naturalism, Purposeful Explanation, and Freedom

We begin with the concept of a choice. What is a choice? A choice is an undetermined mental action, and when we make choices we typically explain our making them in terms of reasons, where a reason is a purpose, end, or goal for choosing. A reason is a conceptual entity, what medieval thinkers called an *ens rationis* (literally "object of reason") or intentional object, which is about or directed at the future and optative in mood (expressing a wish that the world be a certain way that is good). To put this point in technical terms, while a reason is not a desire or a belief, its optative character stems from its being grounded in the content of a desire or belief that represents a future state of affairs as good and something to be brought about by a more temporally proximate chosen action of the person who has the desire or belief. An explanation of a choice in terms of a reason or purpose is a teleological explanation.

To illustrate the optative conceptual nature of a reason, consider the case of a businesswoman named Monica who is on her way to a meeting that is important for advancement in her career (Kane 1999, 225). On the way to the meeting she witnesses a mugging in an alley. Monica has two alternatives: she can continue on to her meeting or she can help the victim of the mugging. Let us suppose she chooses to help the victim. She believes that the victim's well-being is being jeopardized and that her returning to help the victim is morally right. In light of this belief, her reason or purpose for acting is expressed optatively as *that she do what is morally right* (which, in terms of the first person, is *that I do what is morally right*), and the teleological explanatory relation is expressed by saying that she chooses to return to help the victim *in order to* achieve or bring about the purpose that she do what is morally right. If Monica had chosen to continue on to the meeting because of her desire that she further her career, the content of her reason for choosing would have been *that she further her career* (which, in terms of the first person, is *that I further my career*). She would have chosen *in order to* achieve or bring about the purpose that she advance her career.

By way of summary, a teleological explanation of a choice to perform an action involves an agent (1) having a belief or a desire in the content of which he conceives of or represents the future as including a good state of affairs that is an end or goal to be brought about or produced; (2) conceiving of or representing in the content of a belief the means to the realization or bringing about of this end, where the means begin with the agent performing an action; and (3) making a choice to perform that action in order to bring about the end.

To further fill out this picture, consider the movements of our fingers right now on the keys of our keyboards as we work on the different chapters of this manuscript. If we have libertarian free will (if we make libertarian choices), then these physical movements of our fingers are ultimately and irreducibly explained teleologically in terms of the purpose that explains our making the choice to write this book, which was that we provide a guide to naturalism along with a critical appraisal. Hence, if the movements of our fingers are ultimately occurring because we made a choice to write this book for a purpose, then we must be *causing* those movements to occur as we write these sentences. In other words, if our ordinary view of ourselves is correct, then each of us as a person must cause events to occur in the physical world in virtue of our choice to write this manuscript for a purpose. If we make libertarian choices that are explained teleologically and carry them out, then there must be irreducible *mental-to-physical* causation. (By "mental" we simply mean any psychological state or activity such as believing, intending, desiring, and so on.)

What is wrong with this understanding of our freedom and explanation in relation to certain events in our physical bodies? The problem is that according to strict naturalism, a scientific examination of the causes of bodily action leaves no explanatory room for anything nonphysical. Scientific explanations must by their very nature be limited to physics, chemistry, and biology. The philosopher Jaegwon Kim argues that a neuroscientist (indeed, any scientist) has a *methodological commitment* to the causal closure of the physical world. We quote Kim at some length:

> You want to raise your arm, and your arm goes up. Presumably, nerve impulses reaching appropriate muscles in your arm made those muscles contract, and that's how the arm went up. And these nerve signals presumably originated in the activation of certain neurons in your brain. What caused those neurons to fire? We now have a quite detailed understanding of the process that leads to the firing of a neuron, in terms of complex electrochemical processes involving ions in the fluid inside and outside a neuron, differences in voltage across cell membranes, and so forth. All in all we seem to have a pretty good picture of the processes at this microlevel on the basis of the known laws of physics, chemistry, and biology. If the immaterial mind is going to cause a neuron to emit a signal (or prevent it from doing so), then it

must somehow intervene in these electrochemical processes. But how could that happen? At the very interface between the mental and the physical where direct and unmediated mind-body interaction takes place, the nonphysical mind must somehow influence the state of some molecules, perhaps by electrically charging them or nudging them this way or that way. Is this really conceivable? Surely the working neuroscientist does not believe that to have a complete understanding of these complex processes she needs to include in her account the workings of immaterial souls and how they influence the molecular processes involved. . . . Even if the idea of a soul's influencing the motion of a molecule . . . were coherent, the postulation of such a causal agent would seem neither necessary nor helpful in understanding why and how our limbs move. . . . Most physicalists . . . accept the causal closure of the physical not only as a fundamental metaphysical doctrine but as an indispensable methodological presupposition of the physical sciences. . . . If the causal closure of the physical domain is to be respected, it seems prima facie that mental causation must be ruled out. (Kim 1996, 131-32, 147-48)

Kim's depiction of causal closure vividly captures the kind of elimination of the mental proposed by Rey and Dennett, whom we cited in chapter 1. Kim formulates the causal closure argument in terms of the soul, because the soul is typically conceived of as an immaterial (nonphysical) psychological substance that purposefully performs mental acts that cause effects in its physical body. Because we will devote the next chapter to the naturalist's arguments against the soul's existence, we will not concern ourselves with its existence here. For the most part, we simply assume in this chapter that causation of physical events by teleologically explained mental events, which is the ultimate target of the causal closure argument, is causation by events involving souls.

Strict naturalism offers no place for any explanation that goes beyond the domain of physics, chemistry, and biology. But if we do dismiss an ultimate appeal to irreducible purposes and reasons, the outcome seems baffling. Consider one more example of movements of our bodies that it is natural to think could ultimately be adequately explained only by reference to mental events, where those mental events are teleologically explained and cause neurons to emit signals. Right now we are tired and feel tight in our backs after typing without interruption for several minutes, so we raise our arms in order to relax. Reference to our activity and our purposes for acting seems not only helpful but also necessary to explain both the movements of our fingers on the typewriter while we are typing and the subsequent motions of our arms when we relax. If we assume that we indirectly cause our fingers and arms to move by directly causing some neural events in the motor sections of our brains, then when we move our fingers and raise our arms for purposes, we must cause initial neural events in our brains that ultimately lead to the movements of those extremities. In other words, ultimately in order to explain adequately (teleologically) the movements of our limbs, there must be causal *openness* in our brains. Kim, however, disagrees. Because the neuroscientist assumes causal closure of the physical world, what she discovers as the explanation for what occurs in our brains and limbs when we type and relax must not and need not include reference to explanatory purposes for acting that are had by us.

What is one to make of the causal closure argument? Searle has pointed out the absurdly high price that a proponent of causal closure must pay in defense of it.

> Physical events can have only physical explanations, and consciousness is not physical, so consciousness plays no explanatory role whatsoever. If, for example, you think you ate because you were consciously hungry, or got married because you were consciously in love with your prospective spouse, or withdrew your hand from the fire because you consciously felt a pain, or spoke up at the meeting because you consciously disagreed with the main speaker, you are mistaken in every case. In each case the effect was a physical event and therefore must have an entirely physical explanation. (Searle 1997, 154)

In essence, Searle's point is that embracing causal closure and the irreducibility of the mental to the physical amounts to *epiphenomenalism* of the latter. Epiphenomenalism is the technical philosophical term for the view that while the physical affects the mental, the mental does not have any effects on the physical. (Some of the classic metaphors for this portrait of persons are that the mental is like the foam created by the sea or like sparks created by a machine.) That, indeed, is a hard pill to swallow. It is especially difficult to embrace when one seeks to account for the activity of science itself. Presumably, the explanation of Kim's neuroscientist (like all scientists) pursuing her scientific inquiry is ultimately teleological in nature in the form of a purpose such as that she discover how the physical world works and/or that she better the quality of human life.

Because epiphenomenalism is such a hard pill to swallow, some strict naturalists do not accept it but instead advocate a reductive identification of the mental with what is physical. Kim's own thoughts about this matter are instructive at this point. He recognizes the counterintuitive nature of the conclusion of the argument from causal closure, which is that our mental lives have no explanatory role to play in accounting for events in the physical world (our mental lives are explanatorily epiphenomenal). Hence, to preserve an explanatory role for the mental, he believes we should be committed to a reduction of the mental to the physical:

> Mind-to-body causation is fundamental if our mentality is to make a difference to what goes on in the world. If I want to have the slightest causal influence on anything outside me — to change a light bulb or start a war — I must first move my limbs or other parts of my body; somehow, my beliefs and desires must cause the muscles in my arms and legs to contract, or cause my vocal cords to vibrate. Mental causation is fundamental to our conception of mentality, and to our view of ourselves as agents . . . ; any theory of mind that is not able to accommodate mental causation must be considered inadequate, or at best incomplete. . . . Does this mean that we are committed willy-nilly to reductionism? The answer is no: what we have established . . . is a *conditional* thesis, "If mentality is to have any causal efficacy at all — it must be physically reducible." Those of us who believe in mental causation should hope for a successful reduction. (Kim 2005, 152-53, 161, emphasis Kim's)

According to Kim, physical reduction (reduction of the mental to the physical) enables us to preserve our belief that mentality makes a causal explanatory difference. There are, however, serious problems facing such a reduction. The most serious problem is that the mental and physical appear to be irreducibly distinct. There has yet to be a successful form of the identity theory that exhibits how the mental is the very same thing as the physical. Let us briefly consider this problem, and then reexamine the way Kim and other naturalists conceive of the causal closure of the physical world.

The problem with identifying the mental and physical, where the physical is identified as the world as disclosed in physics, chemistry, and biology, is that conscious, mental experiences are not akin to any such physical objects, events, and processes. One can fully observe all the physical features of a person's brain and yet not know the mental state of the subject unless she reports on her experience or we rely on the reports of other subjects who are in similar brain states. In other words, we are able to develop a neuropsychology only when we go beyond pure neurology (brain synapses) and correlate neurological events with mental states. As Colin McGinn notes: "The property of consciousness itself (or specific conscious states) is not an observable or perceptible property of the brain. You can stare into a living conscious brain, your own or someone else's, and see there a wide variety of instantiated properties — its shape, colour, texture, etc. — but you will not thereby see what the subject is experiencing, the conscious state itself" (McGinn 1991, 10-11). Michael Lockwood similarly underscores the apparent unbridgeable gap between the mental and physical.

Let me begin by nailing my colours to the mast. I count myself a materialist, in the sense that I take consciousness to be a species of brain activity. Having said that, however, it seems to me evident that no description of brain activity of the relevant kind, couched in the currently available languages of physics, physiology, or functional or computational roles, is remotely capable of capturing what is distinctive about consciousness. So glaring, indeed, are the shortcomings of all the reductive programmes currently on offer, that I cannot believe that anyone with a philosophical training, looking dispassionately at these programmes, would take any of them seriously for a moment, were it not for a deep-seated conviction that current physical science

32

has essentially got reality taped, and accordingly, *something* along the lines of what the reductionists are offering *must* be correct. To that extent, the very existence of consciousness seems to me to be a standing demonstration of the explanatory limitations of contemporary physical science. (Lockwood 2003, 447, emphasis Lockwood's)

The problem that McGinn and Lockwood have identified is the problem of how Sagan and Crick (cited in chapter 1) can be right about their claims that all there is to being a person is molecular, bodily life. The identification of the mental and physical seems far more radical than any scientific analogies such as water = H_2O and heat = mean kinetic energy. In the case of water one may clearly and decisively grasp the relationship of *constitution:* water is constituted by H_2O. To understand H_2O is to understand water. Similarly to understand heat as molecules in motion is to understand an evident, compositional relationship, unless one is referring to heat as the felt *sensation* of hotness, in which case there is no apparent composition. (The felt sensation of hotness may be brought about by particle velocities and collisions, but it is not identical with such events.) Geoffrey Madell points out the difficulty of using such scientific analogies to identify consciousness (which he refers to as phenomenal states and properties) with physical states.

> That water is H_2O is discovered a posteriori [or by experience], but the identity is fully revealed. There is no such discovery in the case of the claimed identity between neural and phenomenal state; we discover only a correlation. . . . In the case of water, understanding the microstructure enables one to infer the presence of the relevant, watery surface properties. By contrast, no inference from physical to phenomenal properties is possible. Recourse to the paradigm of the necessary identity of water with H_2O is therefore of no avail. The claimed necessary identity of physical and phenomenal states looks as brute as can possibly be. (Madell 2003, 127)

We shall reinforce this difficulty of collapsing the mental and physical in a later section of this chapter, and consider some naturalist replies. In the meantime, let us look again at the argument from causal closure.

Contrary to what Kim argues, there is good reason to think that the argument from causal closure is unsound or flawed. To understand where it goes wrong, let us distinguish between a neuroscientist qua ordinary human being (we assume ordinary human beings embrace what we are calling the natural view of ourselves) and a neuroscientist qua physical scientist. Surely a neuroscientist qua ordinary human being who is trying to understand how and why our fingers move and arms go up while we are typing must and would refer to us and our reasons (purposes) for acting in a complete account of why our limbs move. Must she, however, qua physical scientist, avoid making such a reference? Kim says yes because, qua physical scientist, she must make an assumption about the causal closure of the physical world. As he says elsewhere, "brain scientists will not look outside the physical domain for explanations of neural phenomena. They are not likely to think that it will be scientifically productive to look for nonphysical, immaterial forces to explain neural events" (Kim 2005, 154). Is Kim right about this, and if he is, is such a commitment compatible with a commitment by a physical scientist as an ordinary human being to causal openness? Or must a neuroscientist who as a physical scientist assumes causal closure also assume, if she is consistent, that as an ordinary human being her mention of choices and their teleological explanations is no more than a heuristic device that is necessary for explanatory purposes because of an epistemic gap in her knowledge concerning the physical causes of human behavior?

To answer these questions it is necessary to consider what about physical entities a physical scientist such as a neuroscientist is trying to discover in her experimental work. What Kim's neuroscientist is trying to discover are the capacities of particles or microphysical entities such as neurons to be causally affected by exercised causal powers of other physical entities, including other neurons. For example, the pioneering neuroscientist Wilder Penfield describes in his book *The Mystery of the Mind* how he produced movements in the limbs of patients by stimulating their cortical motor areas with an electrode (Penfield 1975). As Penfield observed the muscle twitches that resulted from stimulation of his patients' brains with an electrode, he had to assume *during his experiments* that the areas of the brains he was studying were causally closed to other causal influences. Without this assumption he could not conclude both that it was the electrode (as opposed, say, to something "behind the scene" such as an empirically undetectable human soul or God) that causally affected the capacities of the relevant neurons to conduct electrical impulses, and that it was the causal impulses of those neurons that causally affected the same capacities of other neurons further down the causal chains to produce the movements of the limbs. There is no reason, however, to think that because Penfield's scientific work required the assumption of causal closure of the areas of the brains he was studying during his experiments that he also had to be committed as a scientist to the assumption that the physical world is *universally* causally closed (closed in *every* context), where universal causal closure entails that the relevant brain (neural) events can *only* be causally produced by events of other physical entities and not instead by mental events of immaterial souls alone when they choose and intend (plan) to act for purposes. That is, there is no reason to think that because a neuroscientist like Penfield must assume causal closure of a delimited area of the brain in the context of his experimental work in order to discover how physical entities causally interact with each other, that he must also be committed as a scientist to the universal explanatory exclusion of mental events that on certain occasions cause the occurrence of events in the physical world. All that a neuroscientist as a scientist must assume is that during his experiments mental events (either of the subjects themselves or of others) are not causally producing the relevant events in the microphysical entities in the delimited areas of the brain he is studying. If a neuroscientist makes the universal assumption that in *any* context events in microphysical entities can only have other physical events as causes and can never be causally explained by mental events and their purposes, then he does so not as a scientist but *as a strict naturalist.*

Though it is not essentially part of our philosophical response to the causal closure argument, it is relevant to note that Penfield himself was not a strict naturalist. Rather, he was a soul-body dualist. So as a scientist he did not at all embrace the causal closure principle for all phenomena. Moreover, some of his data provided reasons for supporting rather than undermining mental-physical interaction. One of the things he noticed in his experimental work was that his patients reported being consciously aware of the distinction between being *agents* and doing things, and being *patients* and having things done to them. Phenomena such as this led him to endorse dualism.

> When I have caused a conscious patient to move his hand by applying an electrode to the motor cortex of one hemisphere, I have often asked him about it. Invariably his response was: "I didn't do that. You did." When I caused him to vocalize, he said: "I didn't make that sound. You pulled it out of me." When I caused the record of the stream of consciousness to run again and so presented to him the record of his past experience, he marveled that he should be conscious of the past as well as of the present. He was astonished that it should come back to him so completely, with more detail than he could possibly recall voluntarily. He assumed at once that, somehow, the surgeon was responsible for the phenomenon. . . . For my own part, after years of striving to explain the mind on the basis of brain-action alone, I have come to the conclusion that it is simpler (and far easier to be logical) if one adopts the hypothesis that our being does consist of two fundamental elements. (Penfield 1975, 76, 80)

One can surmise, then, that had Penfield been presented with the argument from causal closure, he would have found it wanting. And for good reason. In seeking to understand how events of different physical entities affect the capacities of micro-entities such as neurons, a neuroscientist such as Penfield is seeking to learn about properties of physical entities that are essentially *conditional* or *iffy* in nature. A property that is conditional in nature is one specified in terms such as "If such and such is done to object O (e.g., a cause C is exerted on O), then so-and-so will occur to O (e.g., O will move at rate R)." As the Nobel physicist Richard Feynman says, scientific questions are "questions that you can put this way: 'if I do this, what will happen?' . . . And so the question 'If I do it what will happen?' is a typically scientific question" (Feynman 1998, 16, 45). Chalmers's description of basic particles that are studied by physicists nicely captures their iffy nature: "Basic particles . . . are largely characterized in terms of their propensity to interact with other particles. Their mass and charge is specified, to be sure, but all that a specification of mass ultimately comes to is a propensity to be accelerated in certain ways [moved at certain rates] by forces, and so on. . . . Reference to the proton is fixed as the thing that causes interactions of a certain kind that combines in certain ways with other entities, and so on" (Chalmers 1996, 153).

What Chalmers describes as a propensity of a particle to be accelerated is a capacity of it such that *if* it is actualized by an exercised power of another entity (whether physical or nonphysical in nature), the particle will be necessitated to accelerate. There is nothing, however, in the nature of the propensity or capacity of that particle that requires that it be actualized only by purposeless causal events of physical entities so that the physical world is closed to causal influence of mental events of souls choosing and intending to act for reasons. Hence, the actualization of a microparticle's capacity by a mental event on an occasion when a person chooses to act for a reason is not excluded by anything that is discovered in a scientific study of that capacity. And it is precisely on occasions like those involving the movements of our fingers and arms while typing that a neuroscientist will reasonably believe that the microphysical neural impulses that led to those finger movements must ultimately have originated with the mental causal activity of a soul that was choosing to act for a purpose. If a neuroscientist makes the presupposition that microphysical entities can have their capacities actualized *only* by other physical entities and never by choices made by souls for purposes, then he does so as a strict naturalist and not as a scientist.

Our response to the causal closure argument assumes Feynman's and Chalmers's iffy picture of micro-entities that, in addition to being iffy, is also deterministic in the sense that no effect will occur in any micro-entity unless some causal event determines or necessitates that effect to take place. Might there not however be random (nondeterministic) changes in the system of micro-entities as well as the deterministic ones? In other words, while sometimes a neuron fires because it gets deterministic causal input from the neurons with which it is connected, at other times it fires at random (without any deterministic cause), perhaps as a result of random quantum fluctuations in a chaotic system that are magnified at the neuronal level. Contemporary physics has given us some reason to be open to a host of such possibilities not envisioned in classical physics. An instructive entry in the current *Oxford Companion to Philoso-*

phy cautions materialists about assuming a stable, fully deterministic spatiotemporal realm: "Photons and neutrons have little or no mass and neither do fields, while particles pop out of the void, destroy each other, and pop back again. All this, however, has had remarkably little effect on the various philosophical views that can be dubbed 'materialism,' though one might think it shows at least that materialism is not the simple no-nonsense, tough-minded alternative it might once have seemed to be" (*Oxford Companion to Philosophy* 1995, 530). So, let us not assume a classical (deterministic) Newtonian world, but entertain a brute indeterminacy among the brain's 100 billion neurons.

If we assume for the sake of discussion that neurons do sometimes fire randomly, is it possible to distinguish sharply between random firings and those that occur as the result of being causally determined by a mental event of a person or soul? After all, the two kinds of firings are alike to the extent that neither has a physically deterministic cause. We believe it is possible to make this sharp distinction, and the way to make it is in terms of *context*. All one need do is ask how plausible it is to maintain that every time a person purposefully chooses to do something such as move his fingers to type, an initial neuron just happens to fire at random (as a result of quantum fluctuations, etc.) with the result that finger movements occur that perfectly mesh with or map onto those that are intended by that person. Because such repeated coincidences would literally be, dare we say, miraculous, the only plausible view is that the neuron must not be firing randomly but because of the causal input from a person choosing to act for a purpose.

The discussion to this point makes clear that it is thoroughly reasonable to believe that there can be *gaps* (causal openness) in the course of events in the physical world such that there is room for the explanation of some physical events in terms of a person's causal activity that is ultimately explained teleologically by a purpose. To further clarify the relevance of what we have called the "iffy" nature of a capacity's actualization, consider the following argument for the nonexistence of explanatory gaps (causal closedness) developed by Ted Honderich (Honderich 1993). Honderich asks us to consider a scenario in which a woman, Juliet, sees her boyfriend, Toby, and subsequently chooses to tell Toby that they should have a child. Honderich then asks how we are to view the neurological events in Juliet that correlate with what may be called the relevant teleological events.

Teleological events	Juliet sees Toby	Juliet chooses to tell Toby about wanting a child	Further teleological events
Neurological events	N1	N2	N3→

What, asks Honderich, is the relationship between the neurological events that we have labeled N1 and N2? For Juliet to have libertarian free will (and for a purpose to be explanatorily efficacious), N2 cannot be the unavoidable (determined) effect of N1 or anything else because its unavoidability will make its correlate teleological event equally unavoidable. According to Honderich, however, it is nothing less than unreasonable to think that N2 can be anything other than unavoidable in relationship to N1 and the physical story that precedes N1. To see why it is supposedly unreasonable to think anything other than this, let N3 and subsequent neural events be those that lead to and include the movements of Juliet's lips when she tells Toby that they should have a child. Is there or is there not an unavoidable connection between N2 and what causally results from it, namely, N3 and the neural and other physical events that follow N3 and yield the movements of Juliet's lips?

> If there is not a very high probability that items like [N2] will be followed by other neural events, then actions [speaking with our lips] we fully and absolutely intend will on too many occasions mysteriously not happen. So the links *after* [N2] have to be pretty tight. But then in consistency so do the neural links *before* [N2]. That is unfortunate, since the theory [of libertarian free will] needs these earlier links to be pretty loose in order for Juliet to be held really responsible for what is tied to [correlated with] [N2], her [choice] to speak [to Toby]. (Honderich 1993, 37)

Can this problem of inconsistency really be dealt with? Honderich believes that the answer is no. The correct response, however, is that there is no problem of inconsistency, because of the iffy nature of a capacity's actualization, which in this instance is the actualization of the capacity of a neuron (N2) to fire. Honderich's own treatment of the concept of causation supports the nonexistence of the alleged inconsistency and the possible existence of explanatory gaps in the physical story. In discussing the nature of causation, he asks the reader to consider the lighting of a match here and now. We quote Honderich at some length:

> When we assume that this event was the effect of the match's being struck, what are we assuming? One good reply is likely to be that it was an event that wouldn't have happened if the match hadn't been struck. On the assumption that the striking was cause and the lighting effect, what is true is that *if the striking hadn't happened, neither would the lighting.* . . . We are inclined to think . . . that something else isn't true of an ordinary striking and lighting. We are reluctant to say that *if or since the match was struck, it lit.* The explanation of our reluctance is that even if the match was struck, had it been wet, it wouldn't have lit. . . . [N]ot only the striking was required for the lighting, but also the match's being dry. That was not all that was required. There had to be oxygen present, and the surface on which the match was struck had to be of a certain kind. . . . An event which caused a certain effect is not necessarily such that all like events are followed by like effects. Not all strikings are followed by lightings. A causal circumstance for a certain effect, on the other hand, really is such that all like circumstances *are* followed by like effects. . . . [G]iven a causal circumstance, whatever else had been the case [e.g., the match's color had been different], the effect would still have occurred. A necessitated event just is one for which there was a circumstance which was such that since it occurred, whatever else had been true, the event would still have occurred. (Honderich 1993, 7-11, emphasis Honderich's)

It is true, as Honderich claims, that *given* a causal circumstance, the effect — the actualization of a capacity — had to occur, and *since* the circumstance occurred, the effect was necessitated to occur. But did the circumstance — in the case of the match, the presence of oxygen, the dryness of the match, the match's being struck, etc. — have to occur?

Was it unavoidable? There is no reason to think so, *unless one has pre-supposed the truth of determinism.* Honderich says that "the causal circumstance for an effect will typically be made up of parts which were also effects themselves. . . . This fact about effects — the fact of what you might call causal chains — is very important to determinism" (11). While for the sake of argument it can be conceded that causal circumstances for effects will typically be made up of parts that were also effects themselves, this fact about causal circumstances is not sufficient for the truth of determinism. This is because what is typical is not necessarily universal. In the causal circumstance involving the match, do we think it was unavoidable that the match be struck? Not in the least. For example, a person might strike a match in virtue of having *chosen* to have a fire in the fireplace for the purpose that he stay warm. He need not, however, have *chosen* to have the fire. He might have chosen to turn up the thermostat instead for the purpose that he stay warm.

What, then, about the causal circumstance that includes N2 and what follows from it (N3, subsequent neural events, and the movement of Juliet's lips)? Was that causal circumstance unavoidable? Did it have to occur? The answer depends upon what one says about the relationship between N2 and its corresponding teleological event (Juliet's choosing to tell Toby about wanting a child). If one believes that this teleological event alone causes N2 (there is no physical cause of N2), then there is no reason to think that N2 had to occur, because there is no reason to think that its corresponding teleological event (cause) had to occur, unless one assumes the truth of determinism. Honderich (or Kim) might respond that it is reasonable to believe that there must be a neural event such as N1 that produces N2. Why, however, should one think that this is the case? After all, N1 could be the cause of Juliet's seeing Toby without also being the cause of N2. Moreover, one can concede that a neuroscientist such as Penfield might discover in his experimental work that actualizations of a neural capacity (neural events like N2) can be produced by stimulation with an electrode or by exercisings of the causal powers of certain other neurons. But why think that every actualization of a neural capacity can be produced only in these ways? Why could not an actualization of a neural capacity (e.g., N2) be caused by an exercising of a mental power (a mental event) alone which is made for a purpose?

There is no reason to think this is the case, unless one begs the question at hand and assumes the causal closure of the physical world.[1] Keith Campbell succinctly captures in ontological terms the main methodological point of this section when he states that "[a] material thing can,

1. Our response to the methodological argument for causal closedness is premised upon acceptance of a conception of causation that Kim (and Honderich) also assumes, which is that causation is a *productive* or *generative* relationship between a cause and its effect (what is often called "efficient causation"). Some have argued that this conception of causation is outdated on the ground that the fundamental laws of physics do not mention causality (Loewer 2001). For example, laws of physics about properties such as mass, electrical charge, and motion are expressed in terms of mathematical relationships. In contrast, the mental properties of minds, what we have termed their mental powers and capacities, are not mathematically representable. Hence, because the fundamental concepts of physics are strictly mathematical and include neither causal productivity nor nonquantifiable powers and their exercise, we have reason to be suspicious of the relevance of the causal powers of souls and the purposes for which they act.

Like Kim, we are not physicists, and therefore, like him, we are hesitant about engaging the present critic for fear that we might appear to be spouting off about matters beyond our intellectual purview. Nevertheless, we find Kim's own responses to this argument about the nature of causation from the perspective of contemporary physics persuasive (Kim 2002), and we summarize two of his points. First, Kim suggests that if there is no productive causation anywhere, then there is no mental causation or human agency of any kind (Kim 2002, 642; Kim's response on behalf of the reality of mental causation appears puzzling until one remembers that he believes mental causation is ontologically reducible to physical causation). This is not only unbelievable, but also seems self-refuting. After all, does not the proponent of the argument that causation is not a productive relation believe that he is trying to *produce* a belief in his listeners or readers that there is no productive causality?

Second, Kim points out that the fact that causality is not mentioned in the fundamental laws of physics, or that the word "cause" does not appear in the statements of these laws, does not show that the concept of productive causation is absent from physics. There are the mathematical laws and our *interpretation* or *understanding* of those laws: "My impression is that disputes about the interpretation of quantum mechanics, for example, are replete with causal concepts and causal considerations; e.g., measurement (as in a measurement 'having an outcome') . . . observation (as having a perturbational influence on the system observed [e.g., an exercise of the power of observation collapses a Schrödinger wave function]), interference, etc. . . . Entries on 'force' in science dictionaries and encyclopedias typically begin like this: 'In dynamics, the physical agent which causes a change of momentum' . . . A force causing a body to accelerate strikes me as an instance of productive causation par excellence" (Kim 2002, 676; one might add that the concept of the mass of an object, when expressed numerically, is typically interpreted as a function of that entity's *resistance* to acceleration by a *force*).

without ceasing to be a material thing, respond to forces other than physical ones. The brain, without ceasing to be material, can act under the influence of an immaterial mind" (Campbell 1980, 17).

Before proceeding to the next section of this chapter, it is important to make clear that if the argument from causal closure is successful, it not only makes it impossible to explain some events in the physical world in terms of the causal activity of human souls and their purposes for acting but also makes it impossible to explain other events in the physical world in terms of the causal activity of God and God's purposes for acting. For example, Douglas Futuyma and Matthew Bagger respectively set forth the implications of causal closure for explanations of certain events in the physical world (e.g., the resurrection of Jesus, the healings performed by Jesus) in terms of God and his causal power:

> Science is the exercise of reason, and so is limited to questions that can be approached by the use of reason, questions that can be answered by the discovery of objective knowledge and the elucidation of natural laws of causation. In dealing with questions about the natural world, scientists must act as if they can be answered without recourse to supernatural powers . . . of God. (Futuyma 1982, 169-70)

> [W]e can never assert that, in principle, an event resists naturalistic [physical] explanation. A perfectly substantial, anomalous event, rather than providing evidence for the supernatural, merely calls into question our understanding of particular laws. In the modern era, this position fairly accurately represents the educated response to novelty. Rather than invoke the supernatural, we can always adjust our knowledge of the natural in extreme cases. In the modern age in actual inquiry, we never reach the point where we throw up our hands and appeal to divine intervention to explain a localized event like an extraordinary experience. (Bagger 1999, 13)

Though God's powers vastly exceed those of a human soul, they are nevertheless the powers of a nonphysical, simple substance whose actions are explained in terms of purposes. Therefore, if the argument from the causal closure of the physical world cannot be satisfactorily answered when it is directed at excluding human souls and their purposes from explaining some events in the physical world, that will mean there is no explanatory room for God and God's purposes. Christian (and other) theists would do well to think twice about conceding the soundness of the causal closure argument as it relates to human souls while at the same time trying to preserve explanatory space for God. Any sophisticated strict naturalist will quickly point out that if the assumption of causal closure is justified, not only does it make it impossible to explain some events in the physical world in terms of human souls and their purposes for acting, but also it makes it impossible to explain other events in the physical world in terms of God's purposes for acting.

Given that the causal closure principle is not only highly at odds with the natural understanding of ourselves as agents but also philosophically dubious, an important naturalist roadblock to theism has been challenged.

Strict Naturalism and Qualia

In the previous section we explained why the argument from causal closure fails to provide a good reason to think that physical events cannot be causally explained by undetermined mental events (choices) of souls, where those undetermined mental events are ultimately explained teleologically in terms of a purpose. Choices are actions of a *mental* kind because they have contents and are explained by purposes in the form of optative *that* clauses. For example, we chose *to write this book* (or *that we write this book*), and did so for the purpose *that we explore and assess different forms of naturalism.* Our mental lives include, however, as Penfield's patients were well aware, more than actions. They include events that happen to us. We are often patients, as opposed to agents, and are passive instead of active. Paradigmatic examples of events with respect to which we are patients are experiences of pain. An experience of pain is what philosophers call a quale. It is an experience with a feel or a way it seems to be to its subject from a first-person point of view. Pain is a certain way of feeling that each person apprehends experientially. To ask whether extreme pain feels extremely painful is odd because extreme pain is feeling extremely painful. Pleasure similarly has an experiential what-it-is-like feeling, or quale. Multiple quale are termed qualia.

Strict naturalists look no more favorably on qualia than they do on libertarian free will, teleological explanations, and the soul's causal activity. The explanation for this disfavor can be provided in a slightly modified story of Frank Jackson's about a hypothetical scientist named Mary (Jackson 1982). For whatever reason, Mary has spent her entire life up until now locked in a room and somehow managed never to experience pain. While locked in the room Mary learned all the physical facts that can be known about pain, including that pain is produced by such and such physical objects that cause so-and-so neural happenings that lead people to utter expletives, etc., etc. Her knowledge is exhaustive. One night Mary is freed from the room and is invited to go bowling for the first time. As she picks up a bowling ball, she accidentally drops it on her foot and blurts out an expletive. She asks her host what she has just experienced, and he informs her that she experienced pain.

Did Mary learn something new about pain? The obvious answer is yes. She learned for the first time what the *intrinsic nature* of pain is. While in the room she learned only about *extrinsic, relational features* of pain. The point of the story about Mary is that there are more facts, namely, psychological/mental facts, than the physical facts as disclosed in the physical sciences and, therefore, that strict naturalism is false. Why couldn't Mary learn from her studies about the intrinsic nature of pain during the time she was in the room? While part of the answer seems to be that the experiential nature of pain (for lack of a better word, the *ouchiness* of pain) can be known only from the first-person perspective that Mary lacked vis-à-vis pain, another part seems to be that physical explanations of the intrinsic natures of things/events about which Mary learned are typically given in terms of part-whole compositional and spatial terms. Take the solidity of the tables on which our computers presently sit. Their solidity vis-à-vis the computers is explained in terms of a lattice structure of microparts held together by attractive bonds that are sufficiently strong to withstand pressures to be split apart that are exerted by objects such as our computers. Such explanations, however, won't work for an experience of pain (or, just as importantly, for the making of a choice) because it is a defining characteristic of this event that it lacks an event structure. That is, an experience of pain is *simple* in nature in the sense that it is not made up of event parts. A baseball game is an event made up of a series of events (pitches, hits, catches, innings), and complex emotions like anger can be made up of parts such as the event of forming a judgment (e.g., that someone has wronged you) and the event of having certain feelings (e.g., one may feel an intense aversion), but a simple case of feeling pain is not a structure composed of subevents. Hence, it cannot be understood in such terms. As McGinn has stated, "Consciousness defies explanation in [compositional, spatial] terms. Consciousness does not seem to be made up out of smaller spatial processes. . . . Our faculties bias us towards understanding matter in motion, but it is precisely this kind of understanding that is inapplicable to the mind-body problem" (McGinn 1991, 18 n. 21).

Given that it is impossible to provide a compositional analysis of the intrinsic nature of an event such as an experience of pain, what is a strict naturalist to do with it? If he restricts himself to the explanatory framework of physics with its categories of mass and energy, it is hard to see how he can do anything other than simply eliminate pain (deny that it exists) or reductively identify it with some physical event (recall Kim's reductive strategy). Those who attempt to persuade us of the plausibility of such an identity usually advocate something like the following.

Suppose that prior to reading this book you had boiled some water for tea and accidentally touched the burner. Other things being equal, you would have experienced pain and withdrawn your hand from the burner, run it under cold water, and iced it for a purpose, namely, that you alleviate the pain and minimize damage to your hand. At least, that is the ordinary view of what would have been going on. What does the strict naturalist, who tries to identify the pain with a physical event, say would have been going on with you and your hand? He often offers a functionalist account in which what is mental or psychological is nothing more than its causal properties: i.e., given that you are not a substantial self or a soul but a mental system, you had (i) a sensor that formed a representation about your environment (that there was a teakettle and burner); (ii) a mental representation of damage to a subregion of your hand; and (iii) a representation of a goal state in which the hand is withdrawn from the burner. Given the event process that involved the representations in (i), (ii), and (iii), and other things being equal, your hand would have been caused to move away from the burner in accordance with the relevant physical laws. Notice, however, that on this functionalist account of what happens when you experience pain, the ouchiness of pain (its subjective feeling) is never mentioned and has simply *disappeared*. All that is left is a system of causal inputs provided by or in the form of representations that produce certain causal outputs. In other words, on the functionalist understanding of an experience of pain, that experience is *exhaustively* characterized in extrinsic, relational terms (inputs and outputs). There is nothing it is like intrinsically to be in pain that is not reducible in a relational analysis to an identity with causes and effects of the pain.

It is precisely the inadequacy of the functionalist characterization of pain that the story about Mary is designed to illustrate. Contrary to what a strict naturalist would have us believe, the fundamental datum provided by an experience of pain is dualistic. When people experience pain, they experience an event of a kind that is intrinsically pure ouchiness and nonrepresentational in nature and that has extrinsic causes and effects. Some of the effects are that people come to have *desires* that they alleviate their pain and *beliefs* that this alleviation is accomplished by withdrawing their limbs. They then form intentions that they withdraw their limbs. Moreover, their experiences of pain do not cause the withdrawal of their limbs. Rather, on the basis of the stated desires and beliefs, people are given purposes or reasons to act, which are that they alleviate their pain and that they minimize damage to their limbs. These purposes then teleologically explain agents forming their intentions to withdraw the limbs, where these intentions causally produce the physical events that ultimately lead to the relevant movements of the limbs to accomplish the stated purposes. (Even if the heat of the burner causes an initial small movement of a person's hand away from it before the experience of pain occurs, this movement is quickly followed by movements whose source is the agent, not the heat of the burner, and which were teleologically explained by the purpose that he alleviate the pain and minimize the damage to his hand.) In short, the fundamental datum is dualistic insofar as there are *two* kinds of mental events, repre-

sentational and nonrepresentational, and *two* kinds of explanations, teleological and causal, neither of which is reducible to the other. Strict
naturalism fails to provide an adequate account of this fundamental datum. Instead, it disregards it.

Not surprisingly, strict naturalists will suggest that we are all being
misled by the story about Mary. For example, a strict naturalist might respond that there is a general principle underlying the Mary argument,
which is that if someone knows a certain body of knowledge but then
learns something new, the subject matter of the new knowledge must be
a feature of reality to which the earlier body of knowledge did not refer.
As a counterexample to this general principle, Andrew Melnyk presents
a different story: "Because of a blow to the head I suffer terrible amnesia
and forget who I am. But I read in the newspaper that tomorrow, for reasons that don't matter, one Andrew Melnyk will be publicly flogged. 'Bad
news for this Melnyk fellow,' I mutter to myself, but I soon return to my
quest to find out who I am. Later, however, I discover that *I* am Andrew
Melnyk, and then, of course, I realize, to my horror, that tomorrow *I* will
be publicly flogged" (Melnyk 2007).

Melnyk says he has acquired new knowledge, but it is false that the
subject matter of the new knowledge is a feature of reality about which
he had no knowledge before discovering that he is Andrew Melnyk. The
subject matter is the same, namely, Andrew Melnyk. What are different
are the two items of knowledge (namely, that of himself and associated
with his use of the first-person pronoun "I" and that of himself and associated with the name "Andrew Melnyk"), where both the pronoun and
the name refer to the same subject but by different representational formats. Melnyk's new knowledge is that he is identical with Andrew
Melnyk. Similarly, Mary's new knowledge about pain does not refer to a
feature of reality to which her scientific knowledge did not refer. Rather,
Mary learns about the identity of what she experiences when she drops
the bowling ball on her foot with the referent of the scientific knowledge
she possessed before leaving the room.

In response, we maintain that the Mary argument does not presuppose the general principle that if someone knows a certain body of
knowledge but then learns something new, the subject matter of the new
knowledge must be a feature of reality to which the earlier body of

knowledge did not refer. Nevertheless, we believe that Mary's new knowledge is not of an identity statement, for two reasons.

First, unlike Melnyk, who while suffering from amnesia continued to have first-person awareness of himself (which was reflected by his use of "I"), Mary had no awareness of how pain feels (what we are calling its ouchiness or subjective feel) before she left the room, which is the period that corresponds to the temporal period when Melnyk suffered from amnesia. Hence, while Melnyk acquires knowledge of an identity between what he took to be two different entities but were really one thing *of which he was previously aware* in two different ways, when Mary leaves the room she becomes acquainted with something (the ouchiness of pain) *of which she was not previously aware.* That of which she was not previously aware is the intrinsic nature of pain. Prior to leaving the room, Mary was aware only of extrinsic, relational features of pain.

Second, if "two" things are in fact one, they must share all their properties in common. However, there is good reason to think that the ouchiness of pain, which is the intrinsic nature of pain, has properties not shared by that about which Mary learns before leaving the room. As we stated earlier, the ouchiness of pain seems to be simple in nature in the sense that it is not made up of event parts (or other structural parts). Physical explanations of the intrinsic natures of things/events are typically given in terms of part-whole compositional relationships. Hence, if Mary learned anything about the intrinsic nature of a physical phenomenon when she learned all the physical facts about pain (again, we suspect she learned about only extrinsic, relational features of pain), then what she learned could not have been about the intrinsic nature of pain.

One other strict naturalist treatment of the story about Mary warrants mention and a brief response. Some strict naturalists claim that what happened to Mary when she dropped the bowling ball on her foot was that she acquired new abilities. For example, Papineau maintains that Mary acquired the abilities to imagine, recall, and reidentify her first experience of pain (Papineau 1993, 106-11). Though there is no reason to contest the claim that Mary acquired the abilities in question, this strict naturalist account of Mary fails for two reasons.

First, the abilities to imagine, recall, and reidentify are all *mental* in nature. Strict naturalists like Papineau simply help themselves to mental abilities that are never mentioned in the hard sciences because they have no home whatsoever in them (Madell 1988, 83).

Second, each of the mental abilities mentioned by Papineau has an internal relational structure in the sense that there is the *event* of imagining or recalling or reidentifying and *what* is imagined or recalled or reidentified. In other words, there are the mental *attitude* and its *content* or *object*. What strict naturalists like Papineau do not make clear is *what* Mary is imagining after her first experience of pain. If our account of the story about Mary is correct, what Mary is imagining is the quale of pain (pure ouchiness), which is something that has completely disappeared in strict naturalist accounts like Papineau's.

The problem Papineau faces is apparent in the claim of Rorty (cited in chapter 1) that we replace the statement "I'm in pain" with reference to a brain state that he formulates as "My C-fibers are firing." The crucial question to ask someone who makes the second claim is: "How does the firing of your C-fibers make you feel?" If Rorty preserves the fact that such and such neurological states make the subject feel pain, then his delineation of brain states only identifies the biological causes of our feeling rather than replaces or eliminates what we know from a first-person point of view: the subjective, conscious awareness of pain and other sensations.

From Strict to Broad Naturalism

While we have addressed some very technical issues and courted a bizarre thought experiment in the previous section, the fundamental thesis we are advancing is straightforward. A narrow form of naturalism that strictly eliminates agency and states of consciousness is too severe. We cited Dennett in chapter 1 as holding that we are more sure of the existence of mass, charge, and space-time than we are of the reality of experience. But according to a very natural understanding of ourselves and science itself, *there would be no knowledge of mass, electric charge, or space-time unless we are enduring selves that have experiences.* The very practice of science itself is unintelligible unless persons exist and have observations and thoughts, and presumably *observing* and *thinking* are experiences. The difficulty with Dennett's attack on consciousness and experience comes to the fore when considering Drew McDermott's defense of Dennett. McDermott thinks that declaring the existence of experience to be basic and indisputable is akin to an insane person declaring he is Jesus Christ. "Suppose a lunatic claims he is Jesus Christ. We explain why his brain chemicals make him think that. But he is not convinced. 'The fact that I am Jesus is my starting point, a brute explanandum [or a not-further-explainable reality]: explaining why I think this is not sufficient [to undermine or discredit the reality of this basic fact].' The only difference between him and us is that he can't stop believing he's Jesus because he's insane, whereas we can't stop believing in phenomenal consciousness because we're not" (McDermott 2001, 147). The analogy is wide of the mark because it radically underestimates the role of consciousness. While one might be able to explain the falsity of one's belief that one is Jesus Christ, one cannot have beliefs at all, either sane or insane, and explanations of or refusals to explain something, unless one is conscious. Hence, explaining away the basic reality of consciousness is not at all like explaining the falsity of a belief. (McDermott's "defense" of Dennett also seems a little odd, because he appears to concede that we are not insane when we acknowledge the existence of consciousness.)

In chapter 1 we cited Dennett's and Dretske's claims that scientific, strict naturalism can supplant our first-person experiential awareness of ourselves. Their claims, however, seem to ignore the simple fact that we cannot have a third-person, "scientific" point of view without having an antecedent first-person awareness. Nicholas Georgalis makes precisely this point in *The Primacy of the Subjective:* "Advocates of a strictly third-person methodology must be implicitly employing data or information gained from their first-person perspective in order that they may have some clue as to what to investigate from a third-person perspective, to even know what is being 'talked about' when subjective states are at issue" (Georgalis 2006, 84).

The stubborn, intractable problem of eliminating or sequestering our experience and mental life in general is the reason most naturalists today accept a broader account of what counts as natural. They acknowledge the reality of consciousness but still mount a strong case against any form of dualism. The soul and God are still off-limits. In the next chapter we take up the naturalist critique of the soul, and then in chapters 4 and 5 consider the naturalist view on values and God.

CHAPTER 3

Naturalism and the Soul

The idea of a soul, as a pure ego or mental substance, persists tenaciously in philosophy.

Anthony Quinton, *The Nature of Things*

In chapter 2 we discussed the strict naturalist's causal closure argument against the reality of a person causally producing effects on occasions when he or she makes undetermined choices that have ultimate and irreducible teleological explanations. We also argued that there is no reason to doubt the reality of conscious experiences of qualia such as pains. Broader forms of naturalism will be our concern in future chapters, but before providing a detailed examination of broader naturalism, we propose defending a belief with which naturalists of all kinds disagree, namely, the existence of the soul as traditionally conceived in dualism.

Strict and broad naturalists disagree fiercely on the existence of consciousness and freedom (witness any of the bitter exchanges in print between Dennett and Searle; see Searle 1997), but their disagreements should not obscure what they all have in common: the rejection of dualism and, as noted in the introduction, theism. In other words, the surface disagreements between individual naturalists should not obscure their profound unity. As the British humorist Michael Frayn observed: "The homogeneity of a group seen from the outside is in inverse proportion to the heterogeneity seen from the inside" or "Likeness is in the eye of the unlike; the like see nothing but their unlikeness" (both cited in the

Penguin Dictionary of Philosophy 1997, s.v. "school"). It is when one steps back from the internal debates between naturalists that one sees the likeness or homogeneity in what they stand against: dualism and theism.

Assessing naturalist views of the dualist understanding of the soul is germane not just because it is the common pet aversion or bête noire of virtually all naturalists, but also because many naturalists wish to preserve some notion of the soul or subject, notwithstanding their privileging the sufficiency of the physical sciences. So Churchland insists that naturalism will preserve some notion of the soul: "One's first impulse, perhaps, is to see the vocabulary and framework of a general theory of the brain as something alien and cold. But it will not be alien if it depicts all of us, at last, as we truly are. . . . Whatever the distractions, we must continue to exercise our reason. And whatever the temptations we must continue to nurture our souls. That is why understanding the brain is so supremely important. It is the engine of reason. It is the seat of the soul" (Churchland 1995, 324). An important question is whether the vocabulary and framework of naturalism is in fact able to provide an accurate account of ourselves. We shall continue to argue in later chapters, as we have concerning strict naturalism in chapter 2, that it cannot, but in this chapter we consider a more limited position: Have naturalists offered convincing reasons to jettison a dualist understanding of human nature? As we shall document in chapter 5, a naturalist argument that dualism is incoherent or obviously wrong is a central premise in the naturalist case against its chief rival, theism. How we assess the naturalist case against dualism is therefore crucial to the overall assessment of naturalism.

Cartesian Souls and Some Preliminary Distinctions

When philosophers see or hear the word "soul," they naturally think of the seventeenth-century philosopher and mathematician René Descartes and what is known as Cartesian dualism. Descartes presented one of the most intellectually compelling dualist conceptions of both the soul and the physical world in the history of thought. While we are not convinced that a dualist must be Cartesian, it will be useful to test the power of naturalism to see whether it has discredited this form of dualism. After we have completed this inquiry, we will consider the idea of non-Cartesian dualism, a view to which we are more intellectually attracted than Cartesian dualism.

What is Cartesian dualism? In general terms, it incorporates the following elements: there are two kinds of substances, each with its essential properties. One kind of substance is a body, and its essential properties include being spatial, extended, divisible into substantive parts, and movable. A second kind of substance is a soul or a mind (we will use these terms interchangeably), and its essential properties include (in addition to mental qualities and qualia) being nonspatial, unextended, indivisible (because it is substantively simple or without parts), and immovable. Because these respective properties are had essentially by their bearers, no entity that has one kind can lose one or more of them and survive to acquire one or more of the other kind. No entity that is a body can become a soul, and vice versa.

If Cartesian dualism is true, there are bodies and there are minds. What makes things especially interesting is that some bodies also *have* minds. According to ultraorthodox Cartesianism, only human bodies have minds. The rest of the animal kingdom contains bodies but no minds. What kinds of bodies other than human have minds is not however important for the topic of this chapter, which is whether it makes any sense to think that an instance of one kind of body, namely, a human body, has a mind, or, stated the other way around, whether it makes any sense to say that a mind has a human body. (As it happens, we do think some nonhuman animals are conscious, feeling, acting beings, and thus, in the vocabulary of Cartesian dualism, we think there are nonhuman animal souls.)

Before we outline and assess the first, most powerful naturalist critiques of dualism, we briefly summarize with a bit more rigor some of our earlier observations about causation. As we understand it, causation is a productive relation that involves (i) a substance and its causal power; (ii) a substance (either the same as or different from that in [i]) and the causal capacity had by it; (iii) a substance's exercising of causal power; and (iv) an actualization by such an exercising of a substance's capacity. Causation consists of the exercise of a causal power by a substance upon itself or another substance, where this exercise of power produces an actualization of a capacity and that actualization is an effect event. A causal power and its corresponding capacity are ontologically irreducible properties that are had intrinsically or per se by a substance or substances.

Consider, now, the following question: Why is this body *my* body? According to the Cartesian dualist, it is not because a person is identical with his body. Rather, it is because of a certain causal relationship in which he stands to it (Descartes 1911, *Meditations,* Meditation VI). Thus, this body is his body because, when it is causally affected, it regularly and directly causes him to have certain experiences (e.g., pain), and when he wills that his body move,[1] his willing directly causes[2] its movement. On this account, were a person regularly to have the experience of pain directly caused by someone else's body or the table on which he is writing when they were causally affected in certain ways, then he would regard either or both of them as his body. Similarly, were his body or the table regularly directly caused to move by his willing its movement, he would regard either or both of them as his body. For most dualists, the union or embodiment of mind and body is so thorough that one naturally treats a person as a functional unity. When we visually see or touch another person, it is not as though we are seeing or touching a mind's container or some kind of vehicle for the mind. Rather, in cases of healthy embodiment, the mind and body function holistically. Only when there is bodily or mental fracturing, the most radical form of which is death, do the mind and body cease to be a unit. So, for many dualists who are also religious, it may be that at death the body gradually ceases to exist while the soul or mind is with God. For most but not all atheist

---

1. On the Cartesian view, the mental action a person performs that causes his body to move is the act of willing or exercising his power of volition. Descartes held this view (Descartes 1970, 235), as does John Foster (Foster 1991, 264). As we understand Cartesian dualism, it need be committed to no more than that a mental event of some kind, whether a willing, a choice, an intention, or something else, is causally productive of an effect event in a physical body. For the sake of discussion, however, we will follow typical Cartesians and talk in terms of willings.

2. The Cartesian dualist says a mind *directly* causes its body's movement to make clear that an entity such as a chair is not (part of) an agent's body because he causes it to move. The chair is not part of an agent's body because its movements are only indirectly caused by him — he indirectly causes it to move by directly causing movement in his body.

dualists, death may mark the cessation or annihilation of the soul or mind, while the body persists temporarily.

We are now ready to consider the naturalist argument against dualism: it cannot account for soul-body interaction.

Causation and Dualism

A Cartesian dualist analyzes what it is for a person's physical body to be his body in terms of causation. Ernest Sosa has acknowledged that this is a promising analysis of ownership until we consider what it is in virtue of which a causal relation obtains (Sosa 1984). According to Sosa, a causal relation obtains only if the appropriate noncausal conditions obtain. Consider the following two examples:

> Someone takes a picture of you, a photograph. Your image is imprinted on a piece of film. The film is imprinted with an image of a face that looks a certain way *because* you have a certain physiognomy. But your physiognomy causes the image on the film only in virtue of the fact that certain conditions hold at a given time with respect to you and the piece of film. The film is in a camera aimed in your direction, and you and the camera are not too far apart, there are not obstacles obstructing the line of sight, you are facing the camera at the time, and there is enough light, and so on; and it is only in virtue of the fact that these conditions all hold that your facial appearance causes the image on the film. . . .
>
> Take another example. A karate expert hits a board and splits it in two. The board splits in two *because* of the blow by the man. And if this is so it is presumably in virtue of certain noncausal conditions that hold at the time, including the board's thickness; its composition; the angle, speed, and force of the blow, etc. And it seems quite evident, moreover, that if anything noncausally a perfect twin of that board, is hit by anyone noncausally a perfect twin of that man, with a blow exactly like that blow in all noncausal respects, then that new board must also split just as did the old, because of the blow. (Sosa 1984, 273, emphasis Sosa's)

Sosa's argument can be filled out as follows: According to the Cartesian dualist, there are many physical bodies and many souls. Consider two souls, named Stewart and Charles, and assume that each chooses at the same time *t* to go to the refrigerator for a Bud Light. Further assume that appropriate movements occur in a body B at *t*+1 and that the willing by Stewart caused those movements in B. What noncausal relation might connect Stewart's willing with the movements in B, where that relation is absent between Charles and B? No spatial relation can do the trick, because souls are not in space and are unable to enter into spatial relations with material objects. Thus, Stewart cannot be closer to B than Charles, or more favorably positioned with respect to B than Charles. Are there any other noncausal properties and/or relations that make it the case that movements in B are causally produced by the willing of Stewart and not Charles? Could it be the noncausal relationship of ownership, so that Stewart and B causally interact because Stewart owns B? But what is the sense of "owns" here? Is it legal or moral? Did Stewart inherit B or earn it as the fruits of his labor? The obvious answer to each of these questions is no.

At this point, says Sosa, Cartesian dualists explicate ownership in terms of direct causal interaction. They tell us that what makes a body such as B the body of a soul such as Stewart is that the two directly causally interact. But if we then ask in virtue of what noncausal relation it is that B and Stewart directly causally interact, the Cartesian dualist is unable to provide us with an answer. The answer cannot be that B and Stewart causally interact in virtue of the fact that B is owned by Stewart, because ownership is supposed to be explained in terms of causal interaction. Moreover, ownership cannot be explained in terms of a certain spatial relation, because Stewart is supposedly not located in space. In the end, it seems as if all that can be said is that B, which is supposedly the body of Stewart, causally interacts with him, period. But this will not do.

> For it is useless to be told that what makes something subject to direct causal interaction with something else is that it is indeed subject to direct causal interaction with it. And that is precisely what the answer by reference to ownership [explained in terms of causation] . . . re-

solves to under analysis. . . . Our picture begins to look bleak for im-
mortal souls. What pairs physical objects as proper mates for causal
interaction is in general their places in the all-encompassing spatial
framework of physical reality. It is their spatial relations that pair the
piece of film with the man photographed, and distinguishes him as
the cause from the billions of other men in existence including exact
look-alikes. One consequence for interactionism is that there can be
no interaction between an immaterial soul and a material body. That
of course has been the view of so many, since Gassendi to the present,
that it is firmly settled as a platitude of introductory philosophy. (Sosa
1984, 274-75, 278)

What can the Cartesian dualist say in response to Sosa's argument?

On Sosa's view, the causal terms (the individual substances) of a
causal relation are not able to enter into such a relation in virtue of any
causal properties they possess intrinsically or per se, but they acquire
their causal properties only by first entering into a noncausal relation
that is, say, spatial in nature. Stated differently, all causal properties are
possessed extrinsically or in dependence upon entrance into a
noncausal spatial relation. This view is very similar to the more general
ontological thesis that substantial entities, including causal agents and
patients, do not possess their numerical identity (they are not the particular things that they are) intrinsically (they are not intrinsically individuated or distinct from other particular things), but rather they possess
their numerical identity in terms of their spatial relations to other subjects (they are extrinsically individuated). On both views, a spatial relation is the primary ontological category, not the substantial objects and
their causal properties that are the terms of the relevant relations.

We believe that Sosa's account of causation is largely mistaken. Just
as a spatial relation is not the individuating principle of the substantial
objects that are its terms, but those objects are intrinsically individuated, so also a spatial relation is not the individuating principle of the
relevant causal properties possessed by the terms of the causal relation,
but these are individuated intrinsically and possessed essentially by
their bearers. Given the causal ontology summarized in the previous section, a causal relation obtains or is primarily a function of the causal

power and capacity of the agent and patient objects respectively. A causal relation obtains when a substance that possesses causal power exercises that power to produce the actualization of a capacity. The power of an agent and the capacity of a patient are ontologically irreducible and intrinsic causal features of those objects. They are not derivative properties. A causal agent has a power to produce an effect, and a patient has the capacity to be affected by a causal agent *before* entering into a causal relation. In Sosa's terminology, what *pairs* the agent and the patient objects in a causal relation is the agent's exercise of its causal power upon the patient, where this exercise of causal power actualizes the respective capacity of the patient. Like the causal properties of which it is a function, the causal relation is irreducible.[3]

In light of these comments about the nature of causal properties, consider Sosa's examples of the board and karate expert and the physiognomy and film. How can these examples be explicated in terms of essential and fundamental causal powers and capacities? With the board and the karate expert, the board has a causal capacity to break that is a function of its thickness and composition. The board's thickness and composition can reasonably be understood as determined by the organization or arrangement of the parts of the board. Each part of the board is immediately spatially related to a contiguous part and has the causal capacity to be split apart from its immediately contiguous part. Therefore, the causal capacity of the board to be split can be explained in terms of the capacities of the parts that compose it to be separated from their respective immediately contiguous parts, where those parts are held in

3. Someone might argue that it is implausible to maintain that a causal power is an essential property of its bearer. For example, while a person has the causal power to raise his arm, it is unreasonable to think that it is an essential property of his. He could lose this property and still remain himself.

A brief comment is in order. As we pointed out in note 1, the Cartesian dualist maintains that an agent has the power to will movements in his physical body. Strictly speaking, an agent does not have the causal power to raise his arm. Rather, he has the causal power to will, where this power can be exercised by the agent with the result that his arm rises. An agent who can no longer raise his arm has not lost his power to will. Such a power is essential to him. What has happened is that for some reason or other (e.g., a physiological problem), the appropriate act of will does not produce the effect of the arm's rising.

certain bonding relationships by their causally attractive powers and capacities. The capacity to be separated or split apart is identical with the capacity to be moved, the capacity to be moved being possessed intrinsically by any body. The capacity to be moved is properly understood as causal in nature in that it is actualized by a causal power. Thus, a capacity to be separated from a contiguous part is actualized by a causal power. If the parts of the board are themselves complex, their capacities to be split apart (moved) will be further explained in the way the original board's capacity to be broken is explained. Therefore, contrary to Sosa, rather than the thickness and composition of the board being noncausal conditions of the board's splitting upon being hit by someone such as the karate expert, they are explicable or analyzable in terms of causal capacities and powers. Finally, with regard to the speed and force of the karate expert's blow, it is plausible to think that these are also causal, not noncausal, features of the movement of the karate expert's arm and hand. The angle of the blow is a spatial relation between the board and the hand's movement.

What about photographic imaging? Accounts of imaging typically describe how reflected light in the form of photons, which are basic packets of *energy,* move through space in waves and leave a latent image on a piece of film. So that it forms a latent image, the film is coated with imaging layers of grains of silver-halide crystals. Chemical substances that are sensitive to the different wavelengths of red, blue, and green light are added to these grains. The chemical substances *bond* or *adhere* to the grains through powers and capacities of attraction and transfer the energy of photons to the latter, which will be released through further chemical reactions in the development of the film. As in the account of the board and the karate expert, the account of photographic imaging is a causal one whose basic categories include micro-entities held together in structural relationships that are explicable in terms of exercised and actualized powers and capacities respectively, where those relationships are altered by the introduction of exercised power that leads to the formation of new structural relationships among those micro-entities.

Enough has been said about these specific examples introduced by Sosa. In general, a causal relation obtains when a causal power is exercised and actualizes a capacity. This is an irreducible relation that cannot be explained in noncausal terms. But is it, nevertheless, a dependent relation in the sense that it cannot obtain unless some other noncausal relation obtains? After all, Sosa could modify his original view and accept everything that we have said about causation up to this point, yet maintain that an agent can exercise its causal power upon a patient only when the two objects are spatially related. In this case, causation would be an irreducible but dependent relation.

We believe that a causal relation is dependent in nature. When there are two objects, one with the causal power to affect the other, these two objects must stand in a noncausal pairing relation such that the patient is *accessible to* the agent's exercised causal power in the sense that it can be causally affected by it. Were no such noncausal pairing relation to obtain, the agent would exercise its causal power without affecting the patient. What is not evident, however, is that this noncausal pairing relation upon which the causal relation depends must be spatial in nature. We conclude this section with an explanation of why this is not obvious.

To begin, it seems false to maintain that standing in a spatial relation is sufficient for standing in a causal relation. While being spatial in this sense imposes the condition that the agent of a causal relation stands in a spatial relation to the patient of that relation, this does not imply, as Sosa suggests, that it is because or in virtue of this spatial relation that the causal agent is causally paired with the affected patient. As we have already explained, they are causally paired in virtue of the agent's exercise of its causal power that is directed upon and actualizes the patient's capacity, and the agent has the power to do this and the patient has the capacity to have this done to it ontologically, if not temporally, prior to their entering into this spatial relation. Thus, if an agent and patient are in space, they will have to be in a spatial relation with each other when they enter into a causal relation. But their being spatially related is not sufficient for their being causally related. They could exist in the spatial relation without being causally related because the one is not exercising its causal power upon the other.

A spatial relation between two objects is not a sufficient condition of a causal relation obtaining between them. Is it a necessary condition, even for objects with the requisite causal powers and capacities? Kim thinks so.

Causal relations must be selective and discriminating, in the sense that there can be two objects with identical intrinsic properties such that a third object causally acts on one but not the other, and, similarly, that there can be two intrinsically indiscernible objects such that one of them, but not the other, causally acts on a third object. We believe that objects with identical intrinsic properties must have the same causal powers or potentials, both active and passive (some would identify the causal powers of an object with the set of its intrinsic properties). However, objects with the same causal powers can differ in the exercise . . . of their powers, vis-à-vis other objects around them. This calls for a principled way of distinguishing intrinsically indiscernible objects in causal situations, and it is plausible that spatial relations provide us with the principal means of doing this. (Kim 2005, 85)

What can the Cartesian dualist say at this juncture? It seems as if the fundamental issue is whether it is possible for a nonspatial object to exist. If such an object can exist, then it is not obvious in strictly a priori or conceptual terms that it cannot interact causally with an object located in space. Moreover, if a person has good reason for believing that he is a soul that is nonspatial in nature, and if he also has good reason to believe that a certain physical body is his in virtue of causally interacting with it, then he has good reason to believe that there must be a noncausal pairing relation in which he stands to his body, where this relation is distinct from yet makes possible the causal interaction between his soul (him) and his body. This is the case, even if he cannot state what this noncausal pairing relation is. This position is different from that which says that "what makes something subject to direct causal interaction with something else is that it is indeed subject to direct causal interaction with it" (Sosa 1984, 274-75).

The all-important question at this point is what reason a person might have for believing that he is a nonspatial entity. As we briefly described above, Descartes and other Cartesians maintain that a body is by definition a physical object and, therefore, extended in space. Given that it is extended in this way, it is divisible into substantial parts. Because a soul is simple in nature in the sense that it is not divisible into such parts, it cannot be extended in space. If a Cartesian dualist has no reason to think that his way of carving up the world is suspect and he also believes that he causally interacts with his physical body, then it seems that he has strong support for his belief in the existence of a noncausal pairing relation between his nonspatial soul and its spatial physical body that makes their causal interaction possible, even if he cannot specify what the requisite noncausal pairing relation is.

In response, Sosa might claim that no Cartesian who (for the reasons cited in the previous paragraph) thinks he is a nonspatial entity can reasonably believe that he causally interacts with a certain physical body, without also having a knowledge of a noncausal pairing relation in which he stands to that body and that makes it causally accessible to him. It seems to us, however, that such a claim is no more obvious than the nonobvious claim that a spatial relation is a necessary condition of causal interaction between two entities. Therefore, if a person is convinced that his reasons for believing that he is a nonspatial entity and that he causally interacts with a physical body are better than any reasons he is given for believing that there can be no noncausal pairing relation between a nonspatial soul and a physical body that makes possible causal interaction between the two, then he will be justified in asserting the existence of such a relation, even though he does not know what it is.

Why Not Locate Souls in Space?

A dualist, however, has another alternative: he could hold that he is a soul located in the same spatial framework as his physical body such that the necessary noncausal pairing relation is provided by the shared spatial framework. Not surprisingly, Kim believes that this non-Cartesian dualist alternative raises more problems than it solves (Kim 2005). In this section we discuss four of his criticisms of the idea of a spatial soul.

The first problem he raises concerns the location of a soul that is in space. At what point in space is it to be found?

> If my soul, as a geometric point, is in my body, it must be either in the top half of my body or its bottom half. If it's in the top half, it must be either in its left or right half, and so on, and we should be able to cor-

ner the soul into as small and specific a region of my body as we like. And why should we locate my soul in my body to begin with? Why can't we locate all the souls of this world in one tiny place, say this pencil holder on my desk, like the many thousand angels dancing on the head of a pin?

It would beg the question to locate my soul where my body, or brain, is on the ground that my soul and my body are in direct causal interaction with each other; the reason is that the possibility of such interaction is what is at issue and we are considering the localizability of souls in order to make mind-body causation possible. (Kim 2005, 89)

Kim's reasoning about how a non-Cartesian dualist begs the question concerning a soul's causal interaction with its body seems to go as follows: if a non-Cartesian dualist is wondering about what makes causal interaction between a soul (Stewart) and a body B possible, then he might think that (because he believes that a cause and its effect must be spatially contiguous) what makes it possible is the fact that Stewart is located where B is located. If he then wonders about what makes it the case that Stewart is located where B is located, he might answer that it is the fact that Stewart causally interacts with B. This answer obviously begs the question, however, because it is the possibility of such interaction that is at issue.

A non-Cartesian dualist need not however be guilty of this question-begging reasoning. The explanation for Stewart's being located in the space where B is located is not that Stewart causally interacts with B. It is simply that that is where Stewart is located. As was pointed out in response to Sosa's argument against Cartesian dualism, the terms of a causal relationship are ontologically prior to that causal relationship. No spatial object acquires its location by being in a causal relationship. Rather, it is able to enter into a causal relationship in virtue of its location. Moreover, a non-Cartesian dualist's reason for thinking that a soul is located in the space occupied by its physical body is simply the fact that that is where it seems to be located. For example, Philip Quinn suggests that because an individual's perceptual perspectives on the physical world are located spatially in his physical body, it is preferable to think that the soul occupies a spatial point inside its physical body, where that spatial point is most likely in its brain (Quinn 1997).[4] Even here, however, there is another alternative. For example, Immanuel Kant endorsed the view often favored by medieval, Scholastic philosophers that the soul is present in its entirety at each point in space where it is natural to locate one of its sensations, which, for all intents and purposes, means that the soul is located in every part of space occupied by its physical body. C. D. Broad summarizes Kant's view as follows:

> Now, as far as empirical facts go, Kant thinks that it would be reasonable to say that a person's soul is present equally at every place at which it would be natural to locate any of his sensations. . . . In general, Kant holds that there is nothing in our experience to support the . . . view that the soul is located at a certain point in the region occupied by the brain. He says that he knows of nothing which would refute the Scholastic doctrine that a person's soul is present as a whole in his body as a whole in every part of it. (Broad 1953, 130, 132)[5]

We will make use of this view of the soul's spatial location when we discuss the next three objections of Kim to locating a soul in space.

4. An opponent might argue that a person's perceptual perspectives are located in his physical body because his perceptions are caused by that body. This objection misses the point, for two reasons. First, even if perception is a causal notion (which is by no means obvious) and a person's physical body is the causal source of his perception, the terms of this causal relation (the person and his body) are ontologically prior to the causal relation. Second, the point presently at issue is whether a person locates his perceptual perspectives where he does *on the basis of a belief that his perceptions are caused by his body.* Someone like Quinn could reasonably deny that this is the case. He could plausibly maintain that a person locates his perceptual perspectives where he does on the grounds that he is directly aware of them being located in that space.

5. Augustine, though he preceded the Scholastics, also held the view that the soul is simultaneously present as a whole in all the parts of its physical body (see Teske 2001). There are analogous views about wholes being present in their entirety in different spatial locations. For example, certain views of the Eucharist in Christian thought assert that the body of Christ is present in its entirety in every part of the consecrated bread (see Stump 1982). Also, certain views of universals hold that a universal, say, a certain shade of red, is present in its entirety in every particular that exemplifies that shade of red. This is the case, even though each particular has a different spatiotemporal location. (See Moreland 2001.)

Kim's second objection to spatializing a soul concerns the noncausal pairing relation, what he calls "the pairing problem," that is required for causal interaction between a soul and its body. "If locating souls in space is to help with the pairing problem, it must be the case that no more than one soul can occupy a single spatial point; for otherwise spatial relations would not suffice to uniquely identify each soul in relation to other souls in space" (Kim 2005, 89). At least two responses to this argument are available to the non-Cartesian dualist.

First, the non-Cartesian could simply concede the point (thus, no more than one soul could be in the space of its physical body at one time) and move on. Kim then asks, "But if . . . the exercise of [souls'] causal powers are constrained by spatial relations, why aren't souls just material objects, albeit of a very special, and strange, kind?" (90). While the issues raised by this question go well beyond the scope of this chapter, a brief comment is warranted. What is nonnegotiable for many dualists, Cartesian and non-Cartesian alike, is the idea that the soul is a substantively simple entity in the sense that it has no parts that are themselves substances. Many dualists historically have es-poused this view,[6] and even contemporary naturalists have labeled the natural view of the self the Simple View of the self (Nagel 1986, 43-45). Given this Simple View, what is at issue is whether locating this simple self in space is sufficient for making it a material entity. We suspect that if a non-Cartesian dualist became convinced of the truth of this sufficiency condition, he would simply concede the point to Kim but continue to maintain that he is a soul, because what is of first impor-tance is the soul's substantive simplicity. We also suspect that Kim would not be appeased by this concession because he would be reluc-tant to concede that the soul is a substantively simple entity. At this point the debate about the soul's substantive simplicity would have to be joined (see Goetz 2005).

The second response to Kim's objection takes the same kind of line taken in answering the issue concerning a noncausal pairing relation as

---

6. E.g., Thomas Reid: "[A]ll mankind place their personality in something that cannot be divided, or consist of parts. A part of a person is a manifest absurdity. . . . A person is something indivisible, and is what Liebnitz calls a *monad*" (Reid 1975, 109).

it applied to nonspatial souls: given that the non-Cartesian dualist has a good reason for thinking that souls exist and are located in the spaces occupied by their physical bodies (in the present context, this reason might be the Kantian consideration that their sensations seem to be located in the spaces occupied by their physical bodies), he is justified in holding that there is a noncausal pairing relation that makes possible causal interaction between one soul and a body but not another soul, which is located in the same space as the first, and that body. He is justified in holding this even if he does not know what that noncausal pairing relation is.

Kim's third argument against non-Cartesian dualism concerns how a spatial soul can have the requisite structure to explain its causal abilities.

[I]f a soul, all of it, is at a geometric point, it is puzzling how it could have enough structure to account for all the marvelous causal work it is supposed to perform and how one might explain the differences between souls in regard to their causal powers. You may say: A soul's causal powers arise from its mental structure, and mental structure doesn't take up space. But what is mental structure? What are its parts and how are the parts configured in a structure? . . . [I]t is unclear how a wholly nonspatial mental structure could account for a soul's causal powers. (Kim 2005, 90)

In response, it is necessary to distinguish between structure or complexity at the level of thinghood or substancehood and structure or complexity at the level of properties. A soul that is by hypothesis substantively simple (without structure or complexity at the level of thinghood) can be structured or complex at the level of properties. Stated differently, a lack of substantive parts is compatible with a multiplicity of properties.[7] This is the case whether a soul is nonspatial or spatial, and if the

7. Cf. Descartes: "For, as a matter of fact, when I consider the mind, that is to say, myself inasmuch as I am only a thinking thing, I cannot distinguish in myself any parts, but apprehend myself to be clearly one and entire. . . . And the faculties of willing, feeling, conceiving, etc. cannot be properly speaking said to be its parts, for it is one and the same mind which employs itself in willing and in feeling and understanding" (Descartes 1911, *Meditations*, Meditation VI).

latter, whether it is confined to a geometric point or located in its entirety at each point in space that it experiences sensations. Furthermore, it is plausible to think, as Kim himself recognizes, that an entity's essential properties include, at least in part, if not in whole, its intrinsic powers and capacities (Kim 2005, 85). Hence, it does not seem the least bit implausible to say that a soul's thinking, choosing, experiencing pain, etc., are explainable in terms of its having the powers to think and choose and exercising them, and its having the capacity to experience pain and its being actualized.

Finally, if we assume for the sake of discussion that a soul occupies the same space as its physical body, Kim asks how it can be that the one does not exclude the other (90). Once again, it seems to us that the non-Cartesian dualist can take the line that if he has a good reason for believing dualism and for believing that he occupies the same space as that occupied by his physical body, he can reasonably believe that there is this kind of joint occupancy, even if he cannot explain how it is possible. He might, however, think that the possibility of joint occupancy has something to do with the way in which the two kinds of entities occupy space. If a physical object occupies a region of space in virtue of each of its substantive parts occupying distinct subregions of that space, and a soul occupies a region of space by being present in its entirety at each point in that space, then perhaps the possibility of joint occupancy of the same region of space is a function of the different ways in which they occupy that space.

Kim believes that a careful consideration of the various questions and puzzles that arise from locating souls in space will lead us to conclude that "whatever answers might be offered to these questions [will] likely look ad hoc and fail to convince" (90). We are inclined to agree with Kim that the answers we have proposed will look ad hoc to nondualists such as he. Anyone like Kim who is persuaded that the physical world is causally closed and the movements of our fingers on the keyboard right now can be completely explained in strictly nonteleological causal terms (see chapter 2) will find it hard to avoid thinking anything else about these answers. At least, we would be surprised if Kim were to think otherwise about these answers given his nonteleological views about human agency.

Conclusion

It seems, then, that dualism (whether Cartesian or non-Cartesian) has more going for it than its critics typically admit. While the nature of the causal relationship between a soul and its physical body is mysterious, it is doubtful that this mystery rises to the level of a decisive objection against dualism. This is not only because of the reasons that support the truth of dualism that we have discussed in this chapter and elsewhere (see Goetz 2005 and Taliaferro 1994), but also because causation of any kind, even among physical objects, is ultimately mysterious. Some philosophers argue cogently that causation among physical objects will ultimately be fundamental. That is, there may be certain causal powers (electric charge or spin) possessed by microparticles that are foundational or intrinsic to the objects themselves and not further accounted for by even more basic powers that underlie and explain the charge or spin. Arguably, if there is any causation at all, some causal powers will turn out to be basic and not derived from more basic powers. If this is not a deeply vexing mystery for physical causation, it should not be one for nonphysical causation.

CHAPTER 4

Naturalism, Consciousness, and Values

*It is a matter of record that outstanding proponents of naturalism,
in our own time as well as in the past, have exhibited an unequaled
and tender sensitivity to the esthetic and moral dimensions of human experience; and they have been not only movingly eloquent
celebrants of the role of moral idealism and of intellectual and esthetic contemplation in human life, but also vigorous defenders of
the distinctive character of these values against facile attempts to
reduce them to something else.*

Ernest Nagel, "Naturalism Reconsidered"

The focus in chapters 1 and 2 was strict naturalism, while in chapter 3 we
considered the strength of the naturalistic critique of dualism. In this
chapter we begin to take stock of broad naturalism.

Broad naturalists acknowledge the reality of both consciousness
(subjective states of awareness and sentience are conscious) and values
(both nonmoral, e.g., the goodness of pleasure, beauty, and knowledge;
and moral, e.g., the goodness of benevolence and patience). Kim aptly
summarizes the goal of broad naturalism: preserve consciousness and
values within a fundamentally physicalist or materialist naturalism.
"The shared project of the majority of those who have worked on the
mind-body problem over the past few decades has been to find a way of
accommodating the mental within a principled physicalist scheme,
while at the same time preserving it as something distinctive — that is,

without losing what we value, or find special, in our nature as creatures with minds" (Kim 1998, 2). We first highlight some of the problems broad naturalism faces with locating consciousness in the natural world. This, in turn, leads us to take stock of the problem of consciousness in light of one's overall philosophical framework. We then consider the challenge of recognizing the authority of normative, moral values in a broad naturalist worldview.

The Problem of Emergence

While broad naturalists share with dualists an appreciation for the inescapable reality of consciousness, they part company with dualists by claiming that consciousness is an emergent biological, physical property. For example, Searle is a broad naturalist who treats consciousness and thinking on a par with the way any of our physical organs produce bodily change. Just as our digestion is produced by intestines, stomachs, enzymes, and so on, and photosynthesis by a plant's interaction with its environment, so also consciousness is produced by our brains: "The relation of consciousness to brain processes is like the relation of the solidity of the piston to the molecular behavior of the metal alloys, or the liquidity of a body of water to the molecular behavior of the H_2O molecules, or the explosion in the car cylinder to the oxidization of the individual hydrocarbon molecules" (Searle 2004, 208). Though Searle proposes that we see consciousness as simply one among many natural physical processes, he nonetheless believes that consciousness is absolutely pivotal to human life.

> Consciousness is such a stunning and mysterious phenomenon that one always feels that the very effort to describe it in ordinary words somehow is not only bound to fail, but the very effort reveals a failure of sensibility. The general character of the relation of consciousness to the brain, and thus the general solution of the mind-body problem is not hard to state: consciousness is caused by microlevel processes in the brain and realized in the brain as higher-level or system feature. But the complexity of the structure itself, and the precise nature of the

brain processes involved remains unanalyzed by this characterization. We are tempted to trivialize consciousness by thinking of it as
just one aspect of our lives; and, of course, biologically speaking, it is
just one aspect, but as far as our actual life experiences are concerned
consciousness is the very essence of our meaningful existence. If Descartes had not already destroyed the meaning of the sentence we
could say "the essence of mind is consciousness." (Searle 2004, 157-58)

What is one to think about the view that consciousness is an emergent biological property? The problem with Searle's locating consciousness as part of the natural world the way photosynthesis is part of the biological world or digestion is part of our intestinal and stomach
anatomy, is twofold in nature.

First, there is the point we made in chapter 2: the physical properties
and events noted by Searle are structurally complex (part-whole in nature), while properties and events of consciousness are not. For example,
once you understand the biology you understand photosynthesis, and
once you study the relevant anatomy you understand digestion. Photosynthesis and digestion do not refer to something different from what
you observe and understand about the relevant physical properties and
events. (The same is true for Searle's other analogies involving the solidity of a piston, the liquidity of water, and the explosion in the car cylinder.
Once you understand the microstructures and the attractive forces
among them, you are well on your way to understanding solidity, liquidity, and explosiveness.) But with consciousness, things are utterly different. As McGinn has stated and we quoted in chapter 2, "Consciousness
defies explanation in [compositional, spatial] terms. Consciousness
does not seem to be made up out of smaller spatial processes. . . . Our faculties bias us towards understanding matter in motion, but it is precisely
this kind of understanding that is inapplicable to the mind-body problem" (McGinn 1991, 18 n. 21). Searle himself is aware that consciousness
exhibits the simplicity (lack of part-whole structure) pointed out by
McGinn: "We are not aware in conscious experience of . . . the dimensions of our conscious experience. . . . Although we experience objects
and events as both spatially extended and of temporal duration, our consciousness itself is not experienced as spatial, though it is experienced as

temporally extended" (Searle 1992, 105, 127). Given that Searle recognizes the dimensionless nature of conscious experience, his claim that the relation between consciousness and brain processes is like that between the solidity of a piston and the molecular behavior of its metal alloys is paradoxical at best.

Second, when it comes to how we know things, nothing you are aware of about the brain, taken in conjunction with your knowledge of anatomy, will give you an understanding of consciousness, unless you have reports from conscious subjects who reliably report their subjective experiences. In part, we advanced this point about how we know things in the thought experiment about Mary in chapter 2. Once you have a correlation between subjective conscious states and anatomy, you can conclude that certain brain activity is at least a sign, if not a cause, of certain mental states. What you are not entitled to conclude on the basis of the correlation alone is that *the subjective conscious states are identical with the anatomy.*

Some broad naturalists think that if you give an extensive, sufficiently complex description of brain anatomical states and human behavior, you can close the gap that seemingly prevents their identity. One such strategy is sometimes called functionalism. The basic idea is that consciousness should be identified as one causal factor among many that account for human behavior and language. If the functional description includes only physical terms, we may be able to dislodge the intuitively forceful objection that consciousness simply is not discoverable in brain and other processes, as described from a third-person point of view. As Alan Allport sees it:

> Like "understanding," like "life," our everyday concept of "phenomenal awareness" denotes . . . a great range of different states of affairs. The important and exacting task that confronts us, therefore, if we are to make any scientific headway with the concept of "consciousness," is to describe, to characterize in functional detail (including, of course, to provide behavioural and/or physiological *criteria* for the identification of), these different phenomena. Only then may we hope to ascertain whether there is, in fact, any identifiable property or properties in common between them. (Allport 1988, 162, emphasis Allport's)

But this broad, extensive project does not seem sufficient. The difference between conscious experience on the one hand and physiology and behavior on the other is not a difference in matters of complexity or scope, but a difference in kind. Jeffrey Gray succinctly articulates the problem that materialist forms of naturalism face in crossing the divide between physiology and behavior on the one side and conscious states on the other. "The reason the problem posed by consciousness seems so acute, at least to nonfunctionalists, is the following: nothing that we know so far about behaviour, physiology, the evolution of either behaviour or physiology, or the possibilities of constructing automata to carry out complex forms of behaviour is such that the hypothesis of consciousness would arise if it did not occur in addition as a datum in our own experience; nor, having arisen, does it provide a useful explanation of the phenomena observed in those domains" (Gray 1995, 660).

The systematic way functionalist and other broad naturalist philosophies fail to appreciate the problem at hand is evident in Marvin Minsky's parody of the line of reasoning we are advancing, along with Gray and others. Minsky likens the problem of explaining how apparent conscious experience may emerge from nonconscious forces to the following fallacious form of reasoning that containment cannot arise from boards of wood: "I'll prove that no box can hold a mouse. A box is made by nailing six boards together. But no box can hold a mouse unless it has some 'containment.' No single board contains any containment since the mouse can walk away from it. And if there is no containment in one board, there can't be any in six boards. So the box can have no containment at all, and the mouse can escape" (Minsky 1985, 28).

Here Minsky radically underestimates the problem of consciousness. In his analogy, containment may not be possessed by any one board, but resistance (sufficient to block a mouse) certainly is. If one board blocks the path of a mouse, a six-sided box is a sufficient cube in three-dimensional space to provide the right container. Containment is a structural property the possession of which can be explained in terms of relations among parts. Consciousness, as we have stressed already, is not this kind of property. Moreover, Minsky's analogy can be refocused to underscore the problem of emergence for naturalism. Some of the properties of the box are intrinsic properties of the parts. For example, if each of the boards is made of wood, the box is made of wood. The problem of consciousness is akin to the problem of explaining how you can get intentionality (or the practice of intentionally making traps) from purely nonintentional forces. We remain radically in the dark about how consciousness might emerge as something physical from nonconscious, nonmental parts.

The difficulty facing broad naturalism here lies not only in the evident distinction between conscious experience and physical processes, but also in the ostensible contingency of the relationship between them. That is, insofar as we do not grasp a necessary relationship between consciousness and the physical world, it appears that we have two properties or things that are only contingently related. It is common today for philosophers to hold a principle called the indiscernibility of identicals. Given that water is H_2O, then whatever is true about water is true about H_2O (to drink water is to drink H_2O). But if something is true of consciousness that is not true of the physiology and various events and processes that are supposed to be identical with consciousness, then consciousness is not in fact identical with the proposed physical phenomena. The problem facing broad naturalism is that it appears you can have the physical phenomena and not have consciousness. Even if the two are always correlated, if there is reason to think you could have one without the other, you have a reason to deny their identity.

Let us consider two efforts by broad naturalists to explain away the apparent contingency of the relationship between our consciousness and our bodily life. One is by Searle, and the second is by Thomas Nagel.

Searle articulates the problem of contingency as a problem of conceivability, logical possibility, and impossibility. If his version of broad naturalism is true, it is impossible that the world be as it is now physically and yet there not be consciousness. But it does seem conceivable that you can have such a physical world yet no consciousness, and thus it appears that consciousness is not identical with the relevant physical phenomena.

Dualists think that they are possessed of a deep insight that justifies dualism. . . . Here is the insight: there must be a distinction between the mental and the physical because once the existence and the trajectories of all the microparticles in the universe are set, then the entire physical history of the universe is determined by the behavior of the microparticles. But it is still conceivable that there could be no conscious states at all. That is, it is logically possible that the physical universe could be exactly as it is, atom for atom, but without consciousness. But in fact it is not logically possible that the physical universe should be exactly as it is, atom for atom, without all of its physical features being exactly as they are. (Searle 2004, 128)

What is at stake here is serious, for if Searle is right, it is not possible for the physical and consciousness to be only contingently related. Let us therefore consider Searle's reply to this argument from conceivability.

The argument is correct in pointing out that a description of the third-person facts does not entail the existence of the first-person facts, and this for the trivial reason that the first-person ontology cannot be reduced to the third-person ontology. But the dualist then wants to conclude that consciousness is in a different realm, that it is something over and above the brain. But that conclusion does not follow. What the dualist leaves out of this thought experiment are the laws of nature. When we imagined the trajectory of the microparticles, we were holding all laws of nature constant. But if we try to imagine the trajectory of the microparticles being the same but minus consciousness then we are cheating in the thought experiment, because we are imagining the microparticles *not* behaving in precisely the way they would behave if they were acting in accordance with all the laws of nature, i.e., in such a way as to cause and realize (first-personal, subjective) conscious states. (129, emphasis Searle's)

Does the thought experiment of imagining the physical world without consciousness involve cheating? We do not think so. The point of the thought experiment is that there is no necessary tie between the conscious states and the microparticles; it is possible for one to exist without the other. Maybe one can stipulate that there is a law of nature that the two are bound together in this world, but does this binding hold across all possible worlds? Or, putting it differently, are the laws of nature

77

in this world necessary with the result that they could not be otherwise? Searle answers in the following way: "Once the laws of nature are included in the description of the physical universe, and they must be included because they are partly constitutive of the physical universe, then the existence of consciousness follows, as a logical consequence of those laws" (129).

But are the laws necessary? There is a difference between claiming: (A) it is necessarily the case that if you are in a world in which it is a law of nature (where "law of nature" designates something exceptionless, viz., no miracles) that consciousness occurs if and only if physical events P occur, then given consciousness, there will be P; and (B) it is necessarily the case that it is a law of nature that consciousness occurs if and only if physical events P occur. (B) is a much stronger claim than (A), and Searle has not given any reason for believing (B) as opposed to (A), and thus no reason for thinking he has explained away the apparent contingency between consciousness and physical events and processes. Simply stipulating that the correlation of consciousness and the physical is a law of nature in this world does not suffice. Moreover, in the following passage Searle seems to concede that there is no necessary link between consciousness and the physical world other than what would be provided by "the laws of nature": "Is it logically possible that there should be physical particles without any consciousness in the universe? The answer is yes. But is it possible that there should be the trajectories of physical particles as they have in fact occurred together with the laws of nature that, among lots of other things, determine those trajectories to cause and realize consciousness, but minus any consciousness? Then the answer is no" (129).

Without an argument that such laws of nature are themselves necessary, Searle has not accounted for the contingency between consciousness and the body. Searle actually explicitly acknowledges the relevant contingency in the following passage: "It is a logical possibility, though I think extremely unlikely, that when our bodies are destroyed, our souls will go marching on. I have not tried to show that this [life after death, the soul existing without the body] is an impossibility (indeed, I wish it were true), but rather that it is inconsistent with just about everything we know about how the universe works and therefore it is irrational to believe it" (132). Even if it is irrational for Searle to believe he will survive physical death, conceding that this kind of survival is a possibility (perhaps it is not irrational to hope for it?) suffices to underscore the contingency of the relationship between consciousness and the physical.

Consider, now, Nagel's broadly naturalistic attempt to address the problem of the apparent contingent relationship between consciousness and what is physical. Like Searle, Nagel both acknowledges the apparent simplicity (lack of part-whole structure) of consciousness or the self (Nagel 1986, chapter 3) and concedes that the mental and the physical appear to be different, and in a contingent, causal relationship. Given our present concepts of the mental and the physical, it appears to Nagel that an identity between the two is profoundly problematic:

> What does seem true is that the concept of a mind, or of a mental event or process, fails to plainly leave space for the possibility that what it designates should turn out also to be a physical thing or event or process, as the result of closer scientific investigation — in the way that the concept of blood leaves space for discoveries about its composition. The trouble is that mental concepts don't obviously pick out things or processes that take up room in the spatiotemporal world to begin with. If they did, we could just get hold of some of those things and take them apart or look at them under a microscope or subject them to chemical analysis. (Nagel 1998, 339)

Nagel correctly contends that showing that the mental and physical are correlated causally is not sufficient to secure identity: "The two may correspond extensionally as you like, but numerical identity requires more than that" (Nagel 1998, 340). Moreover, Nagel recognizes that if they are the same state, it must be impossible for one to exist without the other. Nagel recognizes that little philosophical work is being done by employing terms like "supervenience" to explain the mental-physical relationship when these terms are not themselves to be explicated but treated as brute or primitive:

> I believe that the explanatory gap in its present form cannot be closed — that so long as we work with our present mental and physical con-

cepts no transparently necessary connection will ever be revealed, between physically described brain processes and sensory experience, of the logical type familiar from the explanation of other natural processes by analysis into their physico-chemical constituents. We have good grounds for believing that the mental supervenes on the physical — i.e. that there is no mental difference without a physical difference. But pure, unexplained supervenience is not a solution but a sign that there is something fundamental we don't know. We cannot regard pure supervenience as the end of the story because that would require the physical to necessitate the mental without there being any answer to the question *how* it does so. But there *must* be a "how," and our task is to understand it. An obviously systematic connection that remains unintelligible to us calls out for a theory. (344-45, emphasis Nagel's)

Nagel does not, however, allow that dualism might provide such a theory, e.g., a theory that posits an actual difference between the mental and physical that explains why they appear to be contingently related. He suggests instead that we will eventually come to reconceive the physical world and our mental life in a way that will allow us to recognize that our mental life is part of the physical world and, indeed, essentially so. "I believe," writes Nagel, "it is not irrational to hope that someday, long after we are all dead, people will be able to observe the operation of the brain and say, with true understanding, 'That's what the experience of tasting chocolate looks like from outside'" (338). Nagel believes we need a sufficiently expanded understanding of the composition and nature of the physical world so that it can encompass the mental. He proposes that the ideal theory would show us that what we employ mental and physical concepts to refer to turns out to be the same thing:

What will be the point of view, so to speak, of such a theory? If we could arrive at it, it would render transparent the relation between mental and physical, not directly, but through the transparency of their common relation to something that is not merely either of them. Neither the mental nor the physical point of view will do for this purpose. The mental will not do because it simply leaves out the physiology, and has no room for it. The physical will not do because while it includes the behavioral and functional manifestations of the mental, this doesn't, in view of the falsity of conceptual reductionism, enable it to reach to the mental concepts themselves. The right point of view would be one which, contrary to present conceptual possibilities, included both subjectivity and spatiotemporal structure from the outset, all its descriptions implying both these things at once, so that it would describe inner states and their functional relations to behavior and to one another from the phenomenological inside and the physiological outside simultaneously — not in parallel. The mental and physiological concepts and their reference to this same inner phenomenon would then be seen as secondary and each partial in its grasp of the phenomenon: Each would be seen as referring to something that extends beyond its grounds of application. (351)

It is on the grounds of the possible truth of such an ideal theory that Nagel argues that the appearance of a contingent relationship between consciousness and the body is of no consequence. There only appears to be a contingent relationship between the mental and physical because of the lack of an ideal theory that connects them. We believe, however, that Nagel's stance is too skeptical, as his positing of a conceptual expansion to secure a necessary relationship could be used to undermine many uncontroversial thought experiments and the contingencies they support. Spinoza, for example, held that all events and objects in the cosmos are necessarily where they are; your location and reading this book could not have been otherwise. This necessity, for Spinoza, was not relative to some contingent law of nature but was absolutely strictly a matter of necessity such that there is no other possibility. Arguably, however, we can readily imagine different states of affairs taking place and your never seeing this book because it was never written. The plausibility of imagining alternative contingent states of affairs counts as an objection to Spinoza. He has an argument about why everything is necessary, but if that argument fails (as almost all philosophers agree), then the apparent contingency of observed reality is preserved. Under these conditions it would be implausible to resort to Nagel's strategy that we should place our hope in some radical new unforeseen conceptual change that will confirm Spinoza's extraordinary project. (See Taliaferro 1994, 1997, 2002 for a further defense of using thought experiments in the debate over naturalism.)

Naturalism and Background Beliefs

So far we have drawn attention both to the general broad naturalist attempt to account for the emergence of consciousness as a physical property and to the related effort to explain away the apparent contingency of the relationship between consciousness and the physical world. One of the attractions of strict naturalism is that there is no emergence of this kind for which a naturalistic explanation needs to be provided. If consciousness does not exist, there is no difficulty in explaining its reality. As Churchland points out: "Most scientists and philosophers would cite the presumed fact that humans have their origins in 4.5 billion years of purely chemical and biological evolution as a weighty consideration in favor of expecting mental phenomena to be nothing but a particularly exquisite articulation of the basic properties of matter and energy" (Churchland 1995, 211). But if there are (as we have argued) reasons for thinking that mental phenomena are more than "a particularly exquisite articulation of the basic properties of matter and energy," what follows? Could it be that our origins are exclusively or "purely" chemical and biological? What Alastair Hannay says of physicalism can be said of naturalism: "The attitude of much physicalism [to consciousness] has been that of new owners to a sitting tenant. They would prefer eviction but, failing that, are content to dispose of as much of the paraphernalia as possible while keeping busy in other parts of the house. We should, I think, feel free to surmise that the current picture of consciousness eking out a sequestered life as a print-out monitor or raw feeler fails in a quite radical way to capture the facts" (Hannay 1987, 395).

Implicit in Hannay's comments is the point that naturalists who recognize the irreducible and ineliminable reality of consciousness are nevertheless not prone either to see consciousness as a clue to some transcendent, higher consciousness (as in theism) or to identify consciousness as a fundamental property of matter (as do pan-psychists, who posit an elemental mental life to all or most physical objects). So long as there is not an alternative philosophical framework in which to describe and account for consciousness, broad naturalism will always by default wind up being the most promising alternative, perhaps rivaled only by a general skepticism about the adequacy of any general philosophical worldview.

One needs some notion of what *might* be beyond the natural or physical world to see what might be at stake in loosening or tightening our concept of what counts as natural. Leopold Stubenberg makes the excellent point that if there is no alternative to a materialist form of naturalism, we might as well treat consciousness, qualia, subjectivity, and experience as something that will eventually be incorporated into naturalism even though we currently have little idea of how this might be accomplished (Stubenberg 1998). Along similar lines and despite believing that we have no idea about how to naturalize consciousness because our cognitive equipment is simply not up to the task, McGinn holds that a materialist naturalism is the only real alternative: "It is either eliminativism or miracles or hidden structure. Absolute noumenalism is preferable to denying the undeniable [the reality of consciousness] or wallowing in the supernatural" (McGinn 1991, xii). McGinn's mention of "absolute noumenalism" and "hidden structure" is a reference to strategies that assert but do not provide an explicit, positive account of the link between consciousness and the physical world. But failing a coherent, positive form of broad naturalism, what about "wallowing in the supernatural"? As noted in our introduction, the key unifying theme of all naturalism is the denial of theism. It is time to offer some general observations about theism here, and then turn to broad naturalism and values. (The naturalist critique of theism is our central concern in chapter 5.)

According to theism, the origin and continued existence of the cosmos are explained by the basic or fundamental intentional activity of an omnipotent, omniscient, good being, God. Theists do not see intentionality as something that emerges from an utterly mindless background. Behind the emergence of animal and human consciousness is the antecedent nonemergent consciousness or mind of God. According to theism, then, consciousness is not something queer or anomalous, a "parlor trick." McGinn, however, remains unconvinced: "One wants to insist, consciousness cannot *really* be miraculous, some kind of divine parlor trick. It must fit into the natural order of things somehow. Its relation to matter must be intelligible, principled, law-governed. Naturalism about consciousness is not merely an option. It is a condition of understanding. It is a condition of existing" (McGinn 1991, 47). But in a theistic view of consciousness, there is no parlor trick or discrete miraculous act of God behind the emergence of consciousness. At the heart of "the natural order of things" is a divine consciousness. Human and nonhuman animal consciousness emerges in the physical cosmos through an abiding comprehensive will of God that there be a world of physical and nonphysical objects, properties, and relations. The relations between matter, energy, consciousness, the laws of space-time all stem from an overarching, purposeful, divine activity.

In a theistic metaphysics the materialist reductive proposals of Dennett and others articulated in chapters 1 and 2 are reversed. As noted earlier, for naturalists the key philosophical project of strict naturalism is to locate the mental in the physical world, and this means explaining the mental in terms that are not mental. So, Dennett privileges explanations of nature that are, at base, nonmental and make no use of mental terms like "intelligence" and "purpose." In his view, to achieve an ultimately satisfactory explanation of human intelligence requires that one not invoke ever increasingly intelligent forces in the universe, but rather that one account for it without invoking intelligence. Dennett contends that accounts that still leave intelligence unexplained are question begging: "The account of intelligence required of psychology must not of course be question-begging. It must not explain intelligence in terms of intelligence, for instance by assigning responsibility for the existence of intelligence in creatures to the munificence of an intelligent Creator" (Dennett 1978, 83). By explaining intelligence in categories that do not involve intelligence, one can aim to unify the kinds of accounts used in science. Dualists by comparison seem left with intelligence plus all the rest; the mental appears to dangle: "Only a theory that explained conscious events in terms of unconscious events could explain consciousness at all" (Dennett 1991, 454). And, as we saw in chapter 1, Rey adopts a similar strategy. But why cannot this reasoning be turned on its head and replaced with a view that takes consciousness and purposeful activity as the basis for an explanation of the existence of the cosmos? After all, naturalism will (as we shall see in chapter 5) leave us with no sufficient reason for the existence of the cosmos itself. Bertrand Russell summarized a basic naturalist stance when he said of the cosmos: it is "just there, and that's all" (Russell and Copleston 1964, 175). If naturalism accounts for events within the cosmos but cannot account for the cosmos itself, why not consider a worldview that explains the structure and being of the cosmos itself in a singular teleological reality?

In chapter 5 we will consider the naturalist critique of theism. Suffice it to note here that evaluating the description and explanation of consciousness does require a look at these larger questions about the cosmos itself.

Naturalism and Values

Strict naturalists often get rid of the necessary conditions of morality and value by denying the existence of freedom, consciousness, and a substantial self. As Kim notes, this is not a point to be lightly passed over:

> As everyone knows, consciousness has returned as a major problematic in both philosophy and science.... For most of us, there is no need to belabor the centrality of consciousness to our conception of ourselves as creatures with minds. But I want to point to the ambivalent, almost paradoxical, attitude that philosophers have displayed toward consciousness. . . . [C]onsciousness-bashing still goes on in some quarters, with some reputable philosophers arguing that phenomenal consciousness, or "qualia," is a fiction of bad philosophy. And there are philosophers and psychologists who, while they recognize phenomenal consciousness as something real, do not believe that a complete science of human behavior, including cognitive psychology and neuroscience, has a place for consciousness, or that there is a need to invoke consciousness in an explanatory/predictive theory of cognition and behavior. Although consciousness research is thriving, much of cognitive science seems still in the grip of what may be called methodological epiphenomenalism.

Contrast this lowly status of consciousness in science and meta-physics with its lofty standing in moral philosophy and value theory. When philosophers discuss the nature of the intrinsic good, or what is worthy of our desire and volition for its own sake, the most promi-nently mentioned candidates are things like pleasure, absence of pain, enjoyment, and happiness — states that are either states of conscious experience or states that presuppose a capacity for conscious experi-ence. . . . To most of us, a fulfilling life, a life worth living, is one that is rich and full in qualitative consciousness. . . . It is an ironic fact that the felt qualities of conscious experience, perhaps the only things that ultimately matter to us, are often relegated in the rest of philosophy to the status of "secondary qualities," in the shadowy zone between the real and the unreal, or even jettisoned outright as artifacts of confused minds. (Kim 2005, 10-12)

Because broad naturalists recognize the devastating implications of strict naturalism for what matters most to us, they seek to preserve and provide an account of the reality of values. By far the most popular broad naturalist account of values (nonmoral and moral, aesthetic, political, and economic) appeals to the concept of evolution. Wilson and Michael Ruse are especially forceful in arguing for a thoroughly biological ac-count of values:

Human beings function better if they are deceived by their genes into thinking that there is a disinterested objective morality binding upon them, which all should obey. We help others because it is "right" to help them and because we know that they are inwardly compelled to reciprocate in equal measure. What Darwinian evolutionary theory shows is that this sense of "right" and the corresponding sense of "wrong," feelings we take to be above individual desire and in some fashion outside biology, are in fact brought about by ultimate biologi-cal processes. (Ruse and Wilson 1986, 179)

On the view of Ruse and Wilson, there is no higher standard of objective values than biological fitness on which to ground normative standards. The radical contingency of values is brought out in their concession that if evolutionary fitness favored acts we now find cruel, then such "cruelty" would become morally right: "[It is] easy to conceive of an alien intelligent species evolving rules its members consider highly moral but which are repugnant to human beings, such as cannibalism, incest, and love of darkness and decay, parricide, and the eating of feces. . . . Ethical premises are the peculiar products of genetic history, and they can be understood solely as mechanisms that are adaptive for the species which possess them. . . . No abstract moral principles exist outside the particular nature of individual species" (186).

Dawkins similarly sees biological evolution as key to understanding values, though he is more cautious than Wilson and Ruse in his enthusiasm for evolutionary ethics per se. The case of Dawkins is especially interesting. Like Wilson and Ruse, he posits an ultimate, naturalistic universe. He therefore concludes, "The universe we observe has precisely the properties we should expect if there is, at bottom, no design, no purpose, no evil and no good, nothing but blind, pitiless indifference. . . . DNA neither knows nor cares. DNA just is. And we dance to its music" (Dawkins 1995, 133). Dawkins advances no illusions that "nature" may be seen as a positive directing force in promoting what we ordinarily see as ethical or valuable: "If Nature were kind, she would at least make the minor concession of anesthetizing caterpillars before they are eaten alive from within. But Nature is neither kind nor unkind. She is neither against suffering nor for it. Nature is not interested one way or the other in suffering, unless it affects the survival of DNA" (Dawkins 1995, 131). Instead of arguing for a view within which nature is a positive force for the good of oneself and others, Dawkins is famous for advancing the idea that nature has given rise to life-forms that are innately selfish. "Humans and baboons have evolved by natural selection. If you look at the way natural selection works, it seems to follow that anything that has evolved by natural selection should be selfish. Therefore we must expect that when we go and look at the behavior of baboons, humans, and all other living creatures, we will find it to be selfish" (Dawkins 1989, 4). The pervasiveness of selfishness means, according to Dawkins, that what we often consider good and valuable cannot be the guaranteed results of biology alone. To illustrate this point, consider the following four passages.

The first text underscores the thoroughness of Dawkins's resolute genetic biology, while the next three indicate his strenuous resistance to an ethic built solely on evolution.

> [The gene] does not grow senile; it is no more likely to die when it is a million years old than when it is only a hundred. It leaps from body to body down the generations, manipulating body after body in its own way and for its own ends, abandoning a succession of mortal bodies before they sink in senility and death. The genes are immortals, or rather, they are defined as genetic entities that come close to deserving the title. (Dawkins 1989, 34)

> Much as we might wish to believe otherwise, universal love and the welfare of species as a whole are concepts that simply do not make evolutionary sense. . . . But be warned that if you wish, as I do, to build a society in which individuals cooperate generously and unselfishly towards a common good, you can expect little help from our biological nature. (Dawkins 1989, 2-3)

> As an academic scientist, I am a passionate Darwinian, believing that natural selection is, if not the only driving force in evolution, certainly the only known force capable of producing the illusion of purpose which so strikes all who contemplate nature. But at the same time as I support Darwinism as a scientist, I am passionate anti-Darwinian when it comes to politics and how we should conduct our human affairs. (Dawkins 2003, 10-11)

> We have the power to defy the selfish genes of our birth and, if necessary, the selfish memes of our indoctrination. We can even discuss ways of deliberately cultivating and nurturing pure, disinterested altruism — something that has no place in nature, something that has never existed before in the whole history of the world. We are built as gene machines and cultured as meme machines, but we have the power to turn against our creators. We, alone on earth, can rebel against the tyranny of the selfish replicators. (Dawkins 1989, 200-201)

The result is that while Dawkins enthusiastically promotes a naturalistic, reductive explanation of the development of morality and values, he believes that we now have morality and values to justify resisting our biological urges and natural impulses. The natural world has, in a sense, produced beings that are in a position to critique the natural world. Dawkins's position is some distance from Darwin's. The latter shared the optimistic ideal of progress that was so prevalent among his Victorian contemporaries:

> It must not be forgotten that although a high standard of morality gives but a slight or no advantage to each individual man and his children over the other men of the same tribe, yet then an increase in the number of well-endowed men and an advancement in the standard of morality will certainly give an immense advantage to one tribe over another. A tribe including many members who, from possessing in a high degree the spirit of patriotism, fidelity, obedience, courage, and sympathy, were always ready to aid one another and to sacrifice themselves for the common good, would be victorious over most other tribes; and this would be natural selection. (Darwin 1898, 203)

Darwin might be right, but the difficulty is that a morally desirable outcome would rest on a cooperative or at least serendipitous nature. All of this seems to be a matter of biological contingency. Darwin seemed to be aware of this.

> If, for instance, men were reared under precisely the same conditions as hive-bees, there can hardly be a doubt that our unmarried females would, like the worker-bees, think it is sacred duty to kill their brothers, and mothers would strive to kill their fertile daughters; and no one would think of interfering. Nevertheless, the bee, or any other social animal, would gain, in our supposed case, as it appears to me, some feeling of right and wrong, or a conscience. For each individual would have an inward sense of possessing certain stronger or more enduring instincts . ... an inward monitor would tell the animal that it would be better to (follow) one impulse rather than the other . . . the one would have right and the other wrong. (Darwin 1898, 151-52)

But this optimism seems quite precarious and fails to provide an account of what certainly appears to be a fundamental feature of ethics, namely, normativity. The normativity of morality and values in general may be seen in the course of our ordinary moral reasoning. Typically, when judging some act to be morally wrong, we do not presume that its wrongness consists in our disapproval of the act or in our desire that the act not occur. Rather, we disapprove and desire that the act not occur because we take it to be wrong. We also readily allow that our own attitudes and desires may themselves be wrong. For example, let's say that Darwin's nightmare thought experiment in which humans behaved like bees took place, but the sense of right and wrong or conscience that emerged was thoroughly in accord with the worker-bee ethic: these humans thought it was indeed morally right to kill brothers, mothers, and so on. If morality retains any normativity, surely it is an objective fact of the matter that these creatures are thoroughly corrupt and depraved, even if their survival is enhanced in the process.

The difficulty facing naturalists who seek a sufficient account of ethics in evolutionary biology is akin to a problem facing utilitarianism in ethics. Roughly, utilitarians hold that the morally right act for an agent is what will produce the greatest happiness. (A more refined version is that an act is morally right if and only if no other act is available to the agent that will produce greater happiness, where "happiness" is defined in terms of satisfying preferences.) One of the challenges facing utilitarianism is that we seem to be able to imagine many cases when utilitarianism would lead us to think that acts are morally right that appear to most of us to be morally abhorrent, like torturing or executing a perfectly innocent person, killing depressed people, and systematically deceiving innocent parties. In the most bizarre instance, it has been argued that utilitarianism may make it morally compulsory to raise children in happiness chambers where they are electronically assured of ever increasing levels of pleasure. The utilitarian reply has customarily been to argue that none of these projects is likely in our world to reliably produce the greatest happiness. Perhaps this utilitarian reply is sufficient, but a deeper problem remains. Utilitarianism may be vindicated *as long as these possibilities do not occur,* and some of these scenarios do seem like credible possibilities (not the happiness chamber, but a moral dilemma about torturing the innocent is a far more likely candidate in reality and not just in the imagination). In our view, utilitarianism is faulty to the extent that it cannot condemn actions that seem clearly morally abhorrent when they would produce the greatest pleasure. Similarly, while evolutionary success in survival may not in fact be enhanced by fratricide and infanticide (Darwin's examples), if it were to be improved by such acts, then "No one would think of interfering" (in Darwin's phrase) who grounded his or her ethic on evolutionary biology.

Torbjörn Fagerström puts the problem facing evolutionary ethics as follows:

> The theory of evolution does not contain any independent evaluation about what are good or bad features. Therefore there are no independent scales which one can use to estimate the adaptive value that a certain feature has; this value can only be measured on a scale that is given by the actual environment. Suppose that there is a disease that reduces pheasants' ability to escape the goshawk. Goshawks will then mainly capture those pheasants that have the disease and we can observe that the disease has negative adaptive value for pheasants *in an environment where we can find goshawks.* If one, on the other hand, eliminates all goshawks, then the disease is not any longer a handicap and the number of sick pheasants will therefore increase in a goshawk free environment. But these are neither better nor worse pheasants than the healthy ones; they are merely pheasants that are adapted to live in an environment free from goshawks in the same way that healthy pheasants are adapted to live in an environment where there are goshawks. . . . Darwinism does not provide us with values about whether [a particular state of affairs] is a better or worse state of affairs. Period! (Fagerström, cited in Stenmark 2001, 111-12, emphasis Fagerström's)

Nagel concurs with Fagerström. He submits that ethical reflection has an internal logic of its own. Biology can account for our physiology and such, but when it comes to ethics, more is involved than mere survival: "The usefulness of a biological approach to ethics depends on what ethics is. If it is just a certain type of behavioral pattern or habit, accompanied by some emotional responses, then biological theories can be expected to teach us a great deal about it. But if it is a theoretical inquiry that can be approached by rational methods, and that has internal standards of justification and criticism, the attempt to understand it from outside by means of biology will be much less valuable" (Nagel 1979, 142).

An analogy to logic may be useful here. Can biology account for logic? Perhaps biology can account for the emergence of logicians, but the laws of logic (such as the law of identity: A is A, or everything is itself) are not themselves laws of biology. Holmes Rolston aptly summarizes a widely held position that we need more than evolutionary biology to engage in ethics and overall value theory:

> But science is never the end of the story, because science cannot teach humans what they most need to know: the meaning of life and how to value it. The sciences are as practical as theoretical; science has evident survival value, teaching us how to gain benefits that we desire. But what ought we to desire? Our enlightened self-interest? Our genetic self-interest? More children? More science? The conservation of biodiversity? Sustainable development? A sustainable biosphere? The love of neighbor? The love of God? Justice? Equity? Charity? . . . After science, we still need help deciding what to value; what is right and wrong, good and evil, how to behave as we cope. The end of life still lies in its meaning, the domain of religion and ethics. (Rolston 1999, 161-62)

Naturalistic and Theistic Values

Theism does not have the same difficulty as naturalism on the problem of emergence of consciousness and values, partly because theism does not hold that these emerged from nonconscious, value-less sources. Goodness has always existed in the divine nature, and the goodness in the cosmos is itself part and parcel of a created reality by an all-good God. On this view, harming an innocent person is wrong because it both involves the destruction of that individual's good and is a violation of the sacred divine purpose of creation: the sharing of the experience of goodness. The wrongness is thus not ultimately dependent upon the capricious exercise of God's power (*harming the innocent is wrong because God commands that there be no such harm or God will punish all* wrongdoers), but upon the essential nature of an all-good God who creates and sustains a cosmos intended to be good, and who acts to bring goodness out of evil. A full exploration of this latter point would require deep reflection on the problem of evil. Why is there evil at all if there is an all-good, all-powerful God? Can an all-good, all-powerful God overcome or defeat the evil of the cosmos and bring good and redemption out of horrific evils? We have addressed such concerns elsewhere (Taliaferro 1998; Goetz 2003). But some of what we have undertaken in this short book does indirectly address the problem of evil. Consider two points.

First, if the work of chapter 2 is sound, there are good reasons to believe that the natural view of ourselves is correct and that we have libertarian free agency, where our free choices have irreducible teleological explanations. While not all evil can be readily observed to flow from this free agency, some does come from our own free choices and not from predetermined causes. At this point there is a sharp distinction between theism and forms of naturalism that are deterministic in nature (and most forms of naturalism are deterministic). If naturalistic determinism is true, then all the evil that has occurred was determined to occur by naturalistic causes. Deterministic naturalists may be deeply committed to fighting injustice — indeed, there is no doubt that many self-described naturalistic determinists are profoundly committed to promoting justice and other virtues, as noted by Ernest Nagel, whom we cite at the outset of this chapter. But while theists maintain that evil is an aberration, an unnecessary violation of the natural goodness of the cosmos and its purpose, deterministic naturalists see evil as an essential part of nature, a necessary feature of reality and not at all in violation of the purpose of the cosmos.

A modest second point is worth making. We present our suggestion at first paradoxically: it may be good that there is a problem of evil. According to the view of agency we are defending in this book, people make wise choices when they freely and purposefully choose good ends. It is partly because naturalists like Dawkins, Wilson, and Ruse maintain that all human choices (if they even acknowledge the reality of choices) are ultimately explained by causally deterministic and blind evolutionary processes that they discount theistic teleological explanations. If naturalists were to give credence to libertarian freedom and teleological explanations on the plane of humanity, perhaps they would begin to reassess more constructively intentional, teleological explanations on the plane of the divine. It is at this conjuncture that one can make room for our natural sense that evils should not occur. (Arguably, this natural sense is a result of our grasp of the very concept of evil.) Our experience of outrage over evil is very much supported by the theistic worldview that, in turn, also provides some support for the hope that the God who made and sustains the cosmos for a good purpose will indeed bring a great good out of the evils of this world.

We will not pursue the issue of evil further here, for our more pressing task in the next chapter is to look at the dominant naturalist case against the very intelligibility of theism. According to the naturalists we will be considering, even if theism were to be compatible with all the evil in the cosmos or even with ten times the amount of evil that exists, theism still fails in the naturalistic critique of its fundamental tenets.

Brief Summary of Naturalism on Values

For naturalists like Dennett who do not allow for fundamental, irreducible consciousness and values, the emergence of values is quite mysterious. Dennett describes the process of inquiring into and achieving proper values: "Eventually we must arrive at questions about ultimate values, and no factual investigation could answer them. Instead, we can do no better than to sit down and reason together, a political process of mutual persuasion and education that we can try to conduct in good faith. But in order to do that we have to know what we are choosing between, and we need to have a clear account of the reasons that can be offered for and against the different visions of the participants" (Dennett 2006, 14). Dennett even describes the values that he does adhere to as sacred: "I have sacred values — in the sense that I feel vaguely guilty even thinking about whether they are defensible and would *never* consider abandoning them (I like to think!) in the course of solving a moral dilemma. My sacred values are obvious and quite ecumenical: democracy, justice, love, and truth (in alphabetical order)" (23, emphasis Dennett's). These values are surely shared by theists and naturalists, but in broad or strict naturalism it is not clear how one can establish normative values on the basis of processes that are ultimately thoroughly unconscious, nonnormative, and contingent in nature.

CHAPTER 5

Beyond Naturalism

To know who I am is a species of knowing where I stand. My iden-
tity is defined by the commitments and identifications which pro-
vide the frame or horizon within which I can try to determine from
case to case what is good, or valuable, what I endorse or oppose. In
other words, it is the horizon within which I am capable of taking a
stand.

Charles Taylor, *Sources of the Self*

We come, finally, to the most fundamental tenet of strict and broad naturalism: the falsity of theism. The case against theism is complex, but a
large part of it rests on a philosophy of human nature. Echoing Charles
Taylor's language, naturalists use a philosophy of personal identity to
demarcate the horizon or limits of our lives and values. Anthony
Kenny's argument below is representative of how a critique of theism
can be constructed on the grounds of a substantial account of human
intelligence.

> If we are to attribute intelligence to any entity — limited or unlimited,
> cosmic or extra-cosmic — we have to take as our starting point our
> concept of intelligence as exhibited by human beings: we have no
> other concept of it. Human intelligence is displayed in the behavior of
> human bodies and in the thoughts of human minds. If we reflect on
> the active way in which we attribute mental predicates such as

"know," "believe," "think," "design," "control" to human beings, we realize the immense difficulty there is [in] applying them to a putative being which is immaterial, ubiquitous and eternal. It is not just that we do not, and cannot, know what goes on in God's mind, it is that we cannot really ascribe a mind to God at all. The language that we use to describe the contents of human minds operates within a web of links with bodily behavior and social institutions. When we try to apply this language to an entity outside the natural world, whose scope of operation is the entire universe, this web comes to pieces, and we no longer know what we are saying. (Kenny 2006, 52-53)

In this chapter we will consider some powerful arguments that theism has been completely undermined by such a naturalistic interpretation of human life. The examination of the credibility of naturalism in this chapter will draw on the work of chapters 2 and 3. We begin by comparing naturalist and theistic accounts of consciousness, and subsequently move to correct a common naturalistic caricature of theism. Positive naturalist critiques are then evaluated, and the chapter ends with a look at the role of experience in assessing the cogency of naturalism.

Naturalism, Theism, and Consciousness

As we pointed out in chapter 4, naturalists who acknowledge the existence of consciousness tend to offer an extremely diminished view of the nature and roles of consciousness in the cosmos. In an important recent collection of papers on the argument from design, *God and Design,* the editor, Neil Manson, cites three passages that are quite instructive. The first is from Hume's *Dialogues concerning Natural Religion:*

But allowing that we were to take the operations of one part of nature upon another for the foundation of our judgment concerning the origin of the whole (which never can be admitted), yet why select so minute, so weak, so bounded a principle as the reason and design of animals is found to be upon this planet? What peculiar privilege has this little agitation of the brain which we call thought, that we must make it the model of the whole universe? Our partiality in our own favor does indeed present it on all occasions, but sound philosophy ought carefully to guard against so natural an illusion. (Hume, cited by Manson 2003, 12)

Two points in this quotation from Hume are of special interest to us: the issue of thought and its being a little agitation in the brain, and the matter of the design of the universe. The design of something is the making of it for a purpose, and as we saw in chapter 1, strong naturalism is first and foremost a view that is opposed to teleological explanation that is ultimate and irreducible in nature. Even if, however, broad naturalists were to concede the reality of such explanation, those like Hume would remain skeptical about the logical appropriateness of invoking it to explain the origin of the cosmos. Russell shared Hume's skepticism about this matter, as is evident from the following two passages cited by Manson in which Russell mocks the idea that human consciousness and thought are the result of intelligent design.

Is there not something a trifle absurd in the spectacle of human beings holding a mirror before themselves, and thinking what they behold so excellent as to prove that a Cosmic Purpose must have been aiming at it all along? Why, in any case, this glorification of Man? How about lions and tigers? They destroy fewer animal or human lives than we do, and they are much more beautiful than we are. . . . Would not a world of nightingales and larks and deer be better than our human world of cruelty and injustice and war? (Russell, cited by Manson 2003, 12)

Man, as a curious accident in a backwater, is intelligible: his mixture of virtues and vices is such as might be expected to result from a fortuitous origin. But only abysmal self-complacency can see in Man a reason which Omniscience could consider adequate as a motive for the Creator. The Copernican revolution will not have done its work until it has taught men more modesty than is to be found among those who think Man sufficient evidence of Cosmic Purpose. (Russell, cited by Manson 2003, 13)

In our view, this Humean and Russellian criticism of thought and teleological explanation is ineffectual. We make two points, one in response to each author. First, consider Hume's characterization of thought as a "little agitation of the brain." Hume's remarks are taken from a dialogue in which he is often assumed to be represented by the character who advances the claim, cited above, about thought. Manson is merely following a current convention in attributing it to Hume. It should be noted, however, that Hume himself did not identify thought with a "little agitation of the brain." In fact, Hume believed that thoughts were not physical. Because he adhered to Descartes's ontology (see chapter 3) where what is not physical is not spatial, Hume believed that immaterial thoughts were nonspatial. Even if, however, one affirms as we do that thoughts are immaterial yet spatially located (see chapter 3), the issue of their size is simply irrelevant to questions about the origin of the universe. Thoughts are instances of what philosophers term a "propositional attitude," where a propositional attitude is a mental event or state that has content. For example, each of the following is a propositional attitude: belief, desire, hope, fear, and choice. As a propositional attitude, each can be directed at or contain content. Thus, a person can believe, desire, hope, fear, or choose that such and such is the case, where that such and such is the case is the propositional attitude's content. Right now we desire that our readers learn about naturalism from our book and hope that we have communicated our position clearly.

Given this distinction between a propositional attitude and its content, it is eminently reasonable to respond to Hume in the following way: while it is true that a human thought as, or qua, propositional attitude is minute in the sense that it is an event located in a small region of space (presumably in a person's brain), the content of thought can vary widely in terms of its spatial scope. For example, one might think about something as small as an atom or as vast as the entire cosmos. Moreover, while the referents of the contents of our thoughts (what our thoughts are about) are often about objects located in space, if philosophers like Plato are correct, the contents themselves are not located in space but "populate" a nonspatial realm of conceptual objects. In his last book, one of the most influential philosophers of the last century, Roderick Chisholm, highlighted what might be called the strong, unbounded, virtually limitless power of thought in his analysis of properties. On Chisholm's view, being a property should be analyzed in terms of being possibly "such that it is the content of an act of believing" (Chisholm 1996, 12). This suggests that, in principle, thinking and intentionality (the "aboutness" of thought) can be used to delimit all properties, those that are instantiated (are exemplified by particular objects in our or some other world) as well as those that are not. As Chisholm and Plato well understood, the spatial or nonspatial nature of an object in no way affects its capacity to be referred to in thought. Thus, if God exists, neither his not being located in space (his transcendence) nor his being located in his entirety at more than one point in space at the same time (his immanence) prevents our thought from referring to him.

Second, what about Russell's claim that it is ridiculous to believe that the well-being or good of human beings could be the purpose for which God creates our world? We find nothing silly in the least about this idea. Russell's satirical portrait of humans holding up a mirror to themselves is intended to signify vanity, an unjustified pride in and concern about their own good, but it also stems from and reveals a distinctive self-awareness, a level of reflexive consciousness that is partly constitutive of being a person. While the good of human beings is a topic for a book of its own, some brief thoughts about it here are appropriate. Like the vast majority of thoughtful Christian and other theists down through the ages, we think it is eminently reasonable to hold that the purpose for which God creates each one of us is that we have the possibility of experiencing perfect happiness or beatitude in fellowship with him and others of our own kind. In opposition to Russell, why not think that man will be glorified in the sense we have just noted? While Russell is certainly correct to point out that the cruelty and injustice of this world make clear that this perfect happiness will never be found this side of the grave, what is unreasonable about thinking that it can be had in the life beyond?

Moreover, nothing about the perfectibility of human beings is incompatible with the perfectibility of other elements of the cosmos. Most theists today believe the good at which God aims for his creatures and creation includes far more than the good of human life. In the Christian Scriptures one finds writers like Saint Paul noting that the entire creation figuratively longs eagerly for the perfect happiness of human beings so that it too will be liberated from its decay and corruption (Romans 8:18-25). Thus, it is fair to say that Russell's suggestion that theism presents too narrow and anthropomorphic a picture of God's purposes for the cosmos is mistaken. Philosophical theists have no fear of the full work of the Copernican revolution (as Russell suggests) because they are interested in why there is a cosmos at all in which there can be natural science replete with all its revolutions. They argue that a theistic, teleological explanation is called for to account for the good of there being a cosmos of laws of nature that makes possible nonhuman as well as human life.

It is true, then, that cosmic theistic explanations are stated in terms of a being of limitless knowledge and unsurpassable power. In constructing a theistic metaphysic, we employ the concept of a necessary or noncontingent conscious being of unsurpassable power who creates for purposes. To many naturalists this is a matter of unwarranted projection, but whether a mere projection or discovery, a theistic metaphysic needs to be seen as introducing a comprehensive, powerful, teleological account of the very existence and continuation of nature. If we assume theism, then the purposed final goodness of the cosmos can count as the explanation for why it exists, whereas in naturalism the continuation and character of the cosmos are due to processes that can have no prevision of the end to which they lead. The conflict between naturalism and theism is not a matter of different scientific theories of events *within the cosmos,* but of conflicting overall *philosophies of the cosmos itself.*

Before examining a central naturalistic critique of theism in the next section, we briefly and finally turn our attention to ways in which critics of theism, not theists themselves, advance an unduly anthropomorphic portrait of God. Brian O'Shaughnessy, for example, seems to assume that the God of theism would inevitably need to be imprecise: "Well, four centuries of triumphant advance by the rock-bottom physical science of physics cannot but leave some mark on philosophy. When you can predict the wave length of a spectrum line to eight decimal places, it is rather more difficult to believe that the underlying reality of everything is spiritual, e.g. an immaterial Deity. After all, should a Deity be *so* fastidious?" (O'Shaughnessy 1980, 1:xvii, emphasis O'Shaughnessy's). And McGinn seems to think that theists simply take for granted the existence of God: "The theory takes for granted the existence of the conscious agent who is held to explain the existence of all other conscious agents. But if there is a problem about how the conscious beings we see around us come to exist, there is equally a problem about how the conscious being who creates each of those conscious beings came to exist" (McGinn 1999, 86).

In response, it is necessary to point out that O'Shaughnessy suggests the peculiar position that if there is a God, we should expect the universe to be unspecified, vague, or blurred without having any precise features that are measurable to eight decimal places of some length. Or, alternatively, perhaps if there is a God, God would make only objects that are easily delimited by measurements in whole numbers without any use of fractions. Clearly, the God of classical theism is radically different from O'Shaughnessy's portrait. Traditionally, theists understand God to be unsurpassably great in knowledge and power and hold that God will use this knowledge and power for, as we have already argued, good purposes.

What about McGinn's comment? What is missing here is an appreciation that to entertain theism is to entertain the thesis that there is a being whose properties of omniscience, omnipotence, goodness, and *aseity* (self-existence or necessary, noncontingent existence) are not derived from some other agency or explainable in terms of the laws of nature or enfeebled by internal and external constraints. A classic theistic argument asks us to consider the possibility that there is such a being whose existence is necessary or noncontingent and then look at the world to see whether the features of the world make greater or lesser evident sense, in light of either theism or its most plausible alternative, naturalism. Theists do not "take for granted" that God has always existed. The majority of philosophical theists historically have held that God's existence is, by its very nature, necessary. This thesis has been articulated as God's essence *(what God is)* being the same as God's existence *(that God is)*. According to Aquinas, to conceive of God is to conceive of a reality whose very being cannot but exist.[1] One of the reasons for thinking there

---

1. For a classic statement of God's essential or necessary existence, see Aquinas 1975, 1.22. Some theistic philosophers claim that the reason for God's existence is contained in

is a necessarily existing Creator is from the apparent contingency of the cosmos. It is not possible to develop a cosmological argument (an argument for God's necessary existence from the contingency of the cosmos) in detail here, but an appreciation for the reason behind the argument will afford a better picture of what defines naturalism.

Theists do not advance their philosophy along the lines of scientific hypotheses. In some of the passages cited in the introduction to our book, McGinn and Searle seem to suppose that God's existence should be evident in gravity, electromagnetism, nuclear forces, lumps of matter, rocks, asteroids, and black holes. But philosophical theism takes its key line of reasoning not from such items in the cosmos, but from the cosmos as a whole. Why is there a cosmos of gravity, electromagnetism, and so on? Merely explaining parts of the cosmos in terms of other factors within the cosmos will not do, for so long as all these elements are contingent, we will not have a reply for why there is a cosmos at all.

The futility of explaining contingent, dependent beings in terms of other such beings may be seen in a plausible reply to Hume. Hume contended that if you accounted for each part of the cosmos, you would have an explanation of the whole: "But the *whole*, you say, wants a cause. I answer that the uniting of these parts into a whole . . . is performed merely by an arbitrary act of the mind, and has no influence on the nature of things. Did I show you the particular causes of each individual in a collection of twenty particles of matter, I should think it very unreasonable should you afterwards ask me what was the cause of the whole twenty. This is sufficiently explained in explaining the parts" (Hume 1970, part 9). Consider William Rowe's reply to Hume: "When the existence of each member of a collection is explained by reference to some other member *of that very same collection* then it does not follow that the collection itself has an explanation. For it is one thing for there to be an explanation of the existence of each dependent being and quite another

---

God's nature. For an exposition of this view, see Norman Kretzman 1997. Consider an analogy with necessary truths such as the law of identity (A is A or everything is itself), which many but not all naturalists accept. Arguably, the reason for the necessity of the law of identity is contained in its very nature. For further reflection on divine necessity, see Taliaferro 2005, chapters 4 and 5.

thing for there to be an explanation of why there are dependent beings at all" (Rowe 1975, 264). And if we think of the material objects of our world as governed by physical laws, the search for an account of those laws leads to an explanation in the form of an ultimate, transcendent law-giver. As Richard Swinburne argues:

> For an ultimate explanation we need an explanation at the highest level of why those laws rather than any other ones operated. The laws of evolution are no doubt consequences of laws of chemistry govern-ing the organic matter of which animals are made. And the laws of chemistry hold because fundamental laws of physics hold. But why just those fundamental laws of physics rather than any others? If the laws of physics did not have the consequence that some chemical ar-rangement would give rise to life, or that there would be random vari-ations of offspring from characteristics of parents, and so on, there would be no evolution by natural selection. So, even given that there are laws of nature (i.e. that material objects have the same powers and liabilities as each other), why just those laws? (Swinburne 1996, 60)

What Richard Swinburne and other theists seek is an overriding teleo-logical account of the cosmos as a whole (see also Pruss 2006; Koons 2000; Craig 1993; Taylor 1974). Just as we have traced in this book a differ-ence between strict and broad naturalists, we can make a distinction be-tween strict and broad theists. Strict theists, like their naturalist coun-terparts, seek to explain all of creation (with the possible exception of libertarian free will) in terms of divine agency. The great eighteenth-century idealist George Berkeley — who construed the material world in terms of divinely caused sensations or ideas — would count as a strict idealist. Broad theists like Swinburne fully acknowledge the reality and causal properties of the physical world; they simply go further in offering an account about why there is such a contingent cosmos.

As stated earlier, our goal here is *not* to articulate and defend a fully developed cosmological argument for theism. Our goal instead is to clarify the claims of theism vis-à-vis naturalism. In the next section we address forceful naturalist arguments that seek to rule out theism as incoherent.

A Naturalistic Critique of Theism

Bede Rundle has advanced an argument that theism is incoherent (non-sense or necessarily false). The argument is based on the thesis that our language and concepts that describe and explain intentional action are essentially references to material behavior. This is essentially the same line of reasoning advanced by Kenny, cited at the outset of this chapter. As God is nonphysical, the notion that God can act, hear, or know about the world is necessarily false or incoherent.

> We have no idea what it means to speak of God intervening in the affairs of the world. . . . We may well have to broaden our conception of what this universe contains; why should there not be many species of being more intelligent than us, some of whom make their presence felt locally from time to time? However, such a concession leaves us within the physical universe. The difficulty with a supernatural agent is that it requires one foot in both domains, so to speak. To qualify as supernatural it must be distanced from any spatio-temporal character which would place it in our world, but to make sense to us as explanatory of changes therein it must be sufficiently concrete to interact with material bodies, and the more convincingly a case is made for the former status, the greater the difficulty put in the way of the latter. (Rundle 2004, 10, 27, 28)

Rundle contends that the very notion of nonmaterial perception, knowledge, and so on is incoherent, and he takes particular aim at what he sees as the misuse of language in theistic religion:

> Someone who insists that God, though lacking eyes and ears, watches him incessantly and listens to his prayers, is clearly not using "watch" or "listen" in a sense . . . we can recognize, so while the words may be individually meaningful and their combination grammatical, that is as far as meaningfulness goes: what we have is an unintelligible use of an intelligible form of words. God is not of this world, but that is not going to stop us speaking of him as if he were. It is not that we have a proposition which is meaningless because unverifiable, but we simply

misuse language, making an affirmation which, in light of our understanding of the words, is totally unwarranted, an affirmation that makes no intelligible contact with reality. (Rundle 2004, 11)

Dennett offers a similar objection to theism. He proposes that it is incoherent to suppose that God lacks sense organs and is temporal:

Many contemporary Christians, Jews, and Muslims insist that God, or Allah, being omniscient, has no need for anything like sense organs, and, being eternal, does not act in real time. This is puzzling, since many of them continue to pray to God, to hope that God *will* answer their prayers tomorrow, to express gratitude to God for *creating* the universe, and to use such locutions as "what God intends to do" and "God have mercy," acts that *seem* to be in flat contradiction to their insistence that their God is not at all anthropomorphic. (Dennett 2006, 7)

Jan Narveson also argues that theistic explanations are fundamentally flawed:

It ought to be regarded as a major embarrassment to natural theology that the very idea of something like a universe's being "created" by some minded being is sufficiently mind-boggling that any attempt to provide a detailed account of how it might be done is bound to look silly, or mythical, or a vaguely anthropomorphized version of some familiar physical process. Creation stories abound in human societies, as we know. Accounts ascribe the creation to various mythical beings, chief gods among a sizeable polytheistic committee, giant tortoises, super-mom hens, and, one is tempted to say, God-knows-what. The Judeo-Christian account does no better, and perhaps does a bit worse, in proposing a "six-day" process of creation.

It is plainly no surprise that details about just *how* all this was supposed to have happened are totally lacking when they are not, as I say, silly or simply poetic. For the fundamental idea is that some infinitely powerful mind simply willed it to be thus, and, as they say, Lo!, it was so! If we aren't ready to accept that as an explanatory description — as we should not be, since it plainly doesn't *explain* anything, as distinct from merely asserting that it was in fact done — then where do we go from there? On all accounts, we at this point meet up with mystery. "How are we supposed to know the ways of the infinite and almighty God?" it is asked — as if that put-down made a decent substitute for an answer. But of course it doesn't. If we are serious about "natural theology," then we ought to be ready to supply content in our explication of theological hypotheses just as we do when we explicate scientific hypotheses. Such explications carry the brunt of explanation. Why does water boil when heated? The scientific story supplies an analysis of matter in its liquid state, the effects of atmospheric pressure and heat, and so on until we see, in impressive detail, just how the thing works. An explanation's right to be called "scientific" is, indeed, in considerable part earned precisely by its ability to provide such detail. (Narveson 2003, 93)

We think the objections raised by Rundle, Dennett, and Narveson are of fundamental importance. If they succeed, they would undermine both human and divine agency. We will address Narveson's point briefly, and then offer a longer treatment of Rundle's position. A closer inspection of Rundle's antitheistic argument reveals a central theme in this essay: the close interwoven nature between our philosophy of consciousness and the philosophy of God.

Narveson wants scientific details in how divine agency works. He compares explanations that work (water boils because of molecules in motion) with those that do not (God commanded that there be light and, lo, there was light). But consider an example of human agency: you light a candle to accomplish the purpose that you see your beloved. As we emphasized in chapter 1, most of us assume that such a purpose is truly explanatory. There may be a highly complex physiological story to tell about muscles and brains and so on when a candle is lit for this purpose. But upon reflection, most of us would hold that the purpose that you see your beloved was ultimately the explanation for the mental event that caused an initial event in your brain and whatever effects followed from it to produce the movements of your hands and the lighting of the match and the candle. As we argued in chapter 2, if our ordinary or natural view of ourselves is correct and our purposes are truly explanatory, then teleological explanation is not reducible to (not subject to analysis in terms of) nonteleological causal explanation.

One further observation in response to Narveson is that the physical sciences themselves affirm basic explanations. For example, in contemporary particle physics, objects without mass are posited with primitive charges or spins (fundamental causal powers and/or capacities) that are presumed to be the basic foundations for explaining more complex events. Thus, positing a basic causal power, terrestrial or divine, whose exercise is ultimately explained teleologically, is not ipso facto explanatorily empty.

Rundle's critique of divine agency is linked with his critique of human agency, which is that there is no soul or "inner" mental life that causes "outer" bodily behavior. Rundle says this about a decision:

> It is far from clear that a decision has what it takes to cause anything. Consider the moment of decision. Sometimes this is the moment an act is initiated, as when one decides to speak, not at some future time, but then and there. Here deciding to speak differs from *merely* speaking in that it is speaking subsequent to some uncertainty or hesitation, speaking which follows on weighing up the pros and cons of doing so. In this case the deciding is assimilated into the act in a way that makes it unsuited to being the act's cause. However, this is not the kind of case that the causalist has in mind, but his concern is with occasions when there is a lapse of time between the deciding and the acting, as when you decide you will do your utmost to become famous or to follow a career as a musician. (Rundle 2004, 154)

We simply do not understand how it follows from the fact that speaking takes place after uncertainty or hesitation resolved by a decision (choice) that the decision is assimilated into the act of speaking. As we argued in chapters 2 and 3, we think it is eminently reasonable to hold that a decision (choice) to speak is an internal mental event, an event in a soul, which is causally involved in the production of movements of a speaker's lips (by first producing brain events that in turn lead to the movement of the lips). Moreover, if the decision is to become a musician at some point in the distant future, then that inner decision

109

will lead to the formation of an inner intention, which at the relevant future time will causally lead to the relevant musical movements of the agent's body.

Rundle, however, believes that there are additional difficulties for our inner-outer understanding of the human agent:

> If, as [Hume] and many other philosophers have supposed, the relation between will or desire and action is taken to be causal, we can consider ourselves fortunate in finding that when, say, we want to open a door, at the very least an attempt to open the door ensues, since it is in no way foreign to the notion of cause that such a desire should have issued in a quite different effect, as, say, that of taking off our shoes. But we are not at the mercy of such causal vagaries if the relation is the more intimate one whereby, if the action is free, our desires are made manifest in, rather than being causes of, what we do. (156)

Rundle's point is something like the following. Assume that we have decided to type this chapter and that this decision is an inner event in a soul. Are we not lucky that this decision has led to the movements of our fingers on our keyboards and not to our playing soccer? In response we, like Rundle, think there is an element of mystery involved with how we move our bodies. It is amazing that our decisions to move our fingers regularly lead to the movements of those fingers. Rundle seems to argue that if we cannot explain how this regularity obtains, then there is good reason to deny the reality of our decisions and the rest of our interior mental life so as to eliminate the possibility that causal irregularities might arise. At this point we fail to follow Rundle's reasoning. There is an alternative to his suggestion that seems far more reasonable: do not deny what is obvious, namely, the reality of our inner mental lives, and hope that the kind of irregularity to which he draws our attention never arises. Moreover, there are fascinating advances in contemporary neuroscience that presuppose the reality of our interior mental lives. With the development of sophisticated technology, realistic hopes are being born that paralyzed persons might be able to operate artificial limbs through sensor/chip implants in their brains (or electrodes attached to their scalps) that detect neuronal activity produced by their thoughts and imaginings (Pollack 2004, 2006). The thoughts and imaginings are clearly internal mental actions that causally produce both the neural events and the movements of the artificial limbs.

Rundle's attack on our ordinary conception of human agency as involving an inner soul that causally affects its outer body is ultimately aimed at undermining the idea that God is an immaterial agent who causally creates and interacts with his material universe. It does not follow, however, that if Rundle's critique of human agency fails, then his case against divine agency fails. But as one looks more closely at some of Rundle's other examples, his overall case against theism wavers. Take, for example, his critique of divine agency. He allows that *some* intentional control over remote objects may be imaginable or intelligible, but theism nonetheless faces an "intractable difficulty" with conceiving of the scope and precision of divine causation. Rundle shapes his objection against a proposal that psychokinesis could provide a model for thinking of divine agency:

> Those who believe in the reality of psychokinesis consider it possible to effect changes in the world merely through an act of will — Locke's account of voluntary action, we may note, amounts to regarding it as an exercise of psychokinesis directed at one's own limbs. It is not absurd to suppose that issuing a spoken command should have an effect on things in one's environment, nor even that formulating the command to oneself should likewise have external repercussions. Neural activity associated with such an act could conceivably harness larger forces which impacted upon things beyond the brain. Whether the command is delivered out loud or said to oneself, what is difficult to account for is the specificity of the effect. If a soldier is given the command "Attention!" or "Stand at ease!," his understanding of the words puts him in a position to comply. Even when the words are uttered *in foro interno,* we can imagine that some sort of signal should reach an inanimate object, but a seemingly intractable difficulty remains on the side of the object, which is not possessed of the understanding which would result in its moving to the left when told to move to the left, or rotating when told to rotate. Psychokinesis is not a promising

model for making sense of God's action on a mindless cosmos, and God's supposed role as lawgiver. (Rundle 2004, 157)

Rundle's line of reasoning here is puzzling. He suggests that theistic accounts of God's creative power rest on created beings understanding and then obeying divine commands. Clearly this is wide of the mark, though perhaps Rundle's observation bears on accounts of divine revelation when it is not clear what (or whether) God wills. All that to one side, once Rundle allows that an agent can have causal effects on remote objects (Rundle speaks of "some sort of signal"), why would it be incoherent to imagine that such causal efficacy is irresistible (necessarily if God wills that there is light, there is light) and unsurpassed in specificity? Why suppose that God might be able to set subatomic particles in motion, but not be able to specify whether this be (in reference to some frame of reference) to the right or the left?

Rundle's argument to this point seeks to show that theism, while coherent or not nonsensical, is nevertheless false. Should all argument fail, however, he is prepared to affirm theism's incoherence. For example, Rundle maintains that he has "no idea" about theistic claims: "I can get no grip on the idea of an agent doing something where the doing, the bringing about, is not an episode in time" (77). One may well agree that Rundle does indeed not understand the metaphysical claims he writes about, and yet challenge his charge that others also fail in this respect. Certainly the line (presumably taken from Wittgenstein) that to talk of God seeing requires (grammatically) that God have (literal) eyes seems open to question. We are tempted to ask the question, "Whose grammar?" Anselm of Canterbury and Ralph Cudworth (to pick two remote and otherwise quite different figures) held that God's cognition of the world and all its aspects did not require bodily organs. Perhaps they were mistaken, but it is hard to believe they were merely making a mistake in Latin or English grammar. This is especially true if one adopts Rundle's view of meaning, according to which *we* fix the meaning of "God" and presumably words like "to see" and "eyes." Rundle writes: "As with any other word, the meaning of 'God' is the meaning that our usage has conferred upon it, so what is true of God of necessity — that is, by dint of being required for the applicability of the term — is in principle something of which we know" (101). In the seventeenth-century work *The True Intellectual System,* the first extensive philosophy of religion text in English, did not Cudworth use the terms "God" and "seeing" and "eyes" coherently in claiming that God sees and knows without using eyes? Maybe "our usage" makes the claim problematic, and we now know that it is impossible for there to be a nonphysical, cognitive agent. But what scientific account of (or conceptual investigation of) our eyes, brain, and so on led us to believe that a different form of agency and knowledge is metaphysically impossible? (It would be hard to argue that Cudworth was misusing the term "theism," as it appears that he coined the word in English.)

As for Rundle's repudiation of divine agency, it is interesting that he does not explicitly ground this objection in a form of contemporary physicalism. He writes:

> The idea that an ultimate source of being and becoming is to be found in the purely mental and non-physical is at odds with the conception of mind espoused by most contemporary philosophers. It is commonly held that mental states are to be characterized in terms of their causal role, but since such states are thought to be states of the brain, there is no lessening of a dependence on the physical. This is not a position I wish to invoke. It is doubtless true that we could not believe, desire, or intend without a brain, but any attempt to construe belief and the rest as states of that organ involves a serious mismatch between the psychological concepts and physical reality. Beliefs can be obsessive, unwavering, irrational, or unfounded, but nothing inside anyone's head answers to such descriptions. (Rundle 2004, 76-77)

But given Rundle's (we believe correct) misgivings about the identity between mental and brain states, why be so sure that it is impossible for there to be nonphysical agency and cognition? All the theist needs here is the bare coherence of dualism, not its plausibility. It is at this point that our work in chapter 3 bears directly on the assessment of the naturalist critique of theism. We defended the coherence of dualism. If successful only in that task, there is a reply to Rundle, Dennett, Kenny, and Narveson, all of whom base their critique of theism on the grounds of the incoherence of theism.

The Naturalist Critique of Religious Experience in Context

In closing, it is instructive to consider one last naturalist objection to theism, as this will return us to the debates over consciousness in chapters 2 and 3.

A popular argument for theism appeals to the evidential value of religious experience. Several contemporary philosophers argue that the apparent experience of a transcendent, good reality is some evidence for the existence of God (Alston 1991; Gellman 1997; Swinburne 1991; Frank 1989). Dennett's reason for objecting to this line of reasoning is philosophically interesting. He cites with approval the lament of the anthropologist Rodney Needham about trying to reconstruct and interpret the religious experience of the tribal people in Penan in Borneo:

> I realized that I could not confidently describe their attitude to God, whether this was belief or anything else. . . . In fact, as I had glumly to conclude, I just did not know what was their psychic attitude toward the personage in whom I had assumed they believed. . . . Clearly, it was one thing to report the received ideas to which a people subscribed, but it was quite another matter to say what was their inner state (belief for instance) when they expressed or entertained such ideas. If, however, an ethnographer said that people believed something when he did not actually know what was going on inside them, then surely his account of them must, it occurred to me, be very defective in quite fundamental ways. (Needham 1972, 1-2)

Note, however, what Needham's account commits Dennett to: the reality of his own conscious experiences ("what was going on inside them"). That is, if Needham's account is taken at face value, Dennett, like the members of the tribal people in Penan, has privileged or surer access than others about the contents of his own conscious states, states that in his philosophy of mind he regards with deep suspicion. When it comes to criticizing religious claims, Dennett seems to privilege our self-awareness and inner feelings not available to external verification.

When it comes to interpreting religious avowals of others, *everybody is an outsider.* Why? Because religious avowals concern matters that are beyond observation, beyond meaningful test, so the only thing *any-body* can go on is religious behavior, and, more specifically, the behavior of *professing*. A child growing up in a culture is like an anthropologist who is surrounded by informants whose professings stand in need of interpretation. The fact that your informants are your father and mother, and speak in your mother tongue, does not give you anything more than a slight circumstantial advantage over the adult anthropologist who has to rely on a string of bilingual interpreters to query informants. (And think about your own case: weren't you ever baffled or confused about just what you were supposed to believe? You know perfectly well that *you* don't have privileged access to the tenets of the faith in which you were raised. I am just asking you to generalize the point, to recognize that others are in no better position.) (Dennett 2006, 239, emphasis Dennett's)

We highlight Dennett's strategy partly to underscore a point we made in earlier chapters about the difficulties facing strict naturalists like Dennett. But we also wanted to use this occasion to make a suggestion about how to compare worldviews like naturalism and theism.

We suggest that the choice of worldviews is rarely a purely philosophical or theoretical matter. Often, various experiences are involved. So, for example, Keith Ward offers the following portrait of the kinds of experiences that enter into theistic belief and practice.

Many people, perhaps, most, occasionally experience a sense of something transcendent, something beyond decay and imperfection. . . . Perhaps religious faith begins, for many of us, in such small epiphanies, in "a sense and taste for the Indefinite." It is from such glimpses of a spiritual reality underlying this phenomenal world that one may develop a desire to seek a deeper awareness of it, and, if possible, seek to mediate its reality in the world. If that happens, religious faith is born. Worship and prayer are, basically, ways of deepening this awareness and transforming the self to reflect and mediate the divine spirit. (Ward 1996, 102-3)

Naturalists, too, can lay claim to a rich body of literature that testifies to a wonder in the natural world taken alone and in opposition to references to any transcendent divine reality. So, consider Dawkins's testimony: "The universe is genuinely mysterious, grand, beautiful, awe-inspiring. The kinds of views of the universe which religious people have traditionally embraced have been puny, pathetic, and measly in comparison to the way the universe actually is. The universe presented by organized religion is a poky little medieval universe, and extremely limited" (Dawkins 1996, 75).

We have profound respect for what Dawkins describes as the grand, beautiful, and awe-inspiring nature of the cosmos. Our effort in this short book has not been to challenge that, but to challenge the idea that theism leads one to any of the grotesque, "pathetic" consequences charted by Dawkins and other naturalists. We have suggested instead the respects in which various forms of naturalism lead us to highly limited or problematic philosophies of consciousness, the self, agency, and values. Moreover, we have argued in this chapter that the case for naturalism needs to take a theistic alternative seriously. It will require another, different book to develop this alternative more positively and the respects in which a nonnaturalist, theistic view of the cosmos may be grand, beautiful, and awe-inspiring.

Appendix

The Argument from Reason

As we explained in the introduction, our ordinary view of ourselves includes the idea that we ultimately explain our undetermined choices in terms of purposes. In other words, according to our ordinary understanding of ourselves, our choices have ultimate and irreducible teleological explanations. Chapter 2 included an explanation of how teleological explanations in terms of purposes are mental in nature insofar as purposes are conceptual entities that are optative in mood. To refresh our minds, consider teleological explanation as it applies to our act of choice to acquire information about strict naturalism for the purpose that we come to have knowledge (belief) about either its truth or its falsity. It seems that the choice to acquire this information and knowledge falsifies strict naturalism because the ultimate explanation for the choice is the purpose just stated: that we come to have knowledge about either its truth or its falsity.

Insofar as the example in the previous paragraph concerns belief formation, there is good reason to think that strict naturalism is falsified in a second way, a way not essentially connected with teleological explanation. To help explain what this second way is, recall from chapter 2 that events in our mental lives are of two ultimate and irreducibly distinct kinds, namely, actions and passions, which is a distinction that explains or grounds the difference between our being agents and patients. A belief (or, more strictly, the coming to have a belief) is a mental passion, not an action, and therefore it is something with respect to which one is directly a patient and not an agent. This is the case, even though indirectly the ultimate explanation for the formation of that belief might be an active choice of an intellectual pursuit undertaken for the purpose that one come to have true beliefs about a matter such as strict naturalism.

In many (but not all) cases, believings (formations of beliefs) are causally explained by apprehending (being aware of) and believing mental *contents* such as (a) propositions and (b) the logical entailment relationships that obtain among them. Consider two examples.

First, take the logical entailment relationship known as *modus ponens,* whose form is as follows: If A, then B; A; therefore, B. If one apprehends (is aware) that A implies B (if one apprehends "If A, then B"), and also apprehends A, then one *cannot help* but come to believe that B follows from "If A then B, and A" (which is different from believing B). Thus, upon apprehending *modus ponens,* one is *caused* to believe it, where that believing is *causally explained* by that apprehension.

Second, consider *modus ponens* once again, but now assume that in addition to believing it one also *believes* (in addition to apprehending) the antecedent of the relevant conditional and the conditional. Let us say that A is "Mark proposes to Mary" and B is "Mary accepts." Then, given that one believes both that "If Mark proposes to Mary, then Mary accepts" and "Mark proposes to Mary," then one cannot help but form the belief that Mary accepts. In this case, one's belief that Mary accepts is true is *causally explained* by one's apprehension of and belief that *modus ponens* is true *and* one's belief that both "Mark proposes to Mary" and "If Mark proposes to Mary, then Mary accepts" are true.

If in some cases believings are causally explained by other mental events (apprehensions and other believings) in the way just described, then the explanation of some mental events includes other mental events and there is *mental-to-mental causal explanation.* Strict naturalists (and many other naturalists), however, maintain that the causal explanation of believings can never be other mental events such as apprehensions and other believings. This is because they affirm a principle that is akin to but stronger than the causal closure principle, where the latter states that anything that is physical can be explained only in terms of something else that is physical or not mental. According to this stronger principle, anything, whether physical *or mental,* can be explained only in terms of something that is not mental in nature. Therefore, believings must always be explained causally by events that are not mental in nature.

It seems to us that when it comes to believings, strict naturalism is self-defeating (self-refuting). That is to say, it seems to us that any *argument* for strict naturalism entails the falsity of strict naturalism. Support for the view that strict naturalism is self-refuting begins with the following argument for strict naturalism:

i. Every effect event is caused only by nonmental events (this is just a statement of the stronger principle endorsed by strict naturalism).
ii. Believing that strict naturalism is true is a mental effect event.

Therefore,

iii. Believing that strict naturalism is true is caused only by nonmental events.

Assume, as seems thoroughly reasonable, that the strict naturalist believes that the causal explanation for his believing (iii) is his apprehending (i) and (ii) and believing that they are true. The problem is that if (iii) is true, the strict naturalist's apprehending and believing (i) and (ii) cannot be the causal explanation for his believing (iii) because apprehending and believing (i) and (ii) are mental events. Hence, if strict naturalism is true, it undermines the causal explanation for believing that it is true.

An option for the strict naturalist is to maintain that his belief that strict naturalism is true is a basic belief, where a basic belief is one that is *not explained by any other belief* (though a basic belief could be, and typically is, grounded in one's direct apprehension of some element or aspect of the world). On this view, the strict naturalist believes that strict naturalism is true but not on the basis of any argument. If the belief that strict naturalism is true is a basic belief, then it is not self-refuting in the way that we have suggested.

It seems to us, however, that the strict naturalist is not out of the woods yet, for three reasons. First, if a belief that strict naturalism is true is basic in nature, it cannot be caused by an apprehension (awareness) of the way the world is because this would imply that it has a mental explanation. In short, if a belief that strict naturalism is true is basic, not only is it not caused by another belief but also it is a groundless basic belief (one not explained by an apprehension of the way the world is).

Second, it is part of the ordinary view of ourselves that the causes of many of our believings are apprehensions and other believings of ours. If we think of an ordinary view as a basic belief, then the belief that the direct causes of many of our believings are apprehensions and other believings is basic, where this basic belief is grounded in our apprehending ourselves believing certain things that are caused by apprehensions and other believings. Therefore, a belief that strict naturalism is true cannot also be a basic belief, unless one is willing to countenance that we hold contradictory basic beliefs (the belief that strict naturalism is true and the ordinary view of ourselves). In short, if one believes that strict naturalism is true, then it must be because one is *persuaded by an argument* for its truth, and this implies that the cause of this belief is mental in nature. This, however, is the very kind of explanation that strict naturalism excludes. Hence, strict naturalism is self-defeating.

Third, an implication of strict naturalism is that if apprehensions and believings are real events, then their occurrences must be and always are epiphenomenal in nature. (Recall from chapter 2 that epiphenomenalism is the technical philosophical term for the view that while the physical causally affects the mental, the mental does not causally affect the physical.) While we apprehend and believe things to be certain ways, these apprehensions and believings explain nothing. They are explanatorily impotent. As we also pointed out in chapter 2, epiphenomenalism is indeed a hard pill to swallow.

Let us label the argument of this appendix the argument from reason. Because it is easy to misstate this argument, it is important to make clear what the problem is for strict naturalism. Consider C. S. Lewis's version of the argument from reason, which he sets forth in chapter 3 of the second edition of his book *Miracles*. Lewis claims that the "mere existence of causes for a belief is popularly treated as raising a presumption that it is groundless" (Lewis 1960, 16). To support his claim, Lewis cites a popular way of discrediting what a person believes (showing that the explanation for a person's believing what he does is not a good one), which is to claim that the belief is caused by a person's being a capitalist, a hypochondriac, a mere man, or a woman. Like Lewis, we believe one must be careful here. It is not the mere existence of a cause for a belief that discredits it. Rather, it is the *kind* of cause that discredits it. To discredit what a person believes in the way pointed out by Lewis is to allege that what causes the belief in question is not apprehensions and other beliefs (e.g., the apprehension of and belief in the truth of a logical rule of inference such as *modus ponens* along with a belief that both a conditional and its antecedent are true), but the person's *desire for wealth* or *fear about becoming ill,* neither of which *justifies* or *grounds* the belief. In short, it is the *kind* of cause of a belief and not the mere fact that it has a cause that discredits it. When certain beliefs are causally explained in terms of other beliefs and apprehensions, the efficacy of those causes is essentially related to their *contents* (to *what* is believed or apprehended), which *justify* or *ground* the beliefs in question.

Another important point that Lewis does not explicitly make is that the practice of discrediting a belief in the way he points out *presupposes* that we believe that many of our beliefs can be and often are explained by apprehensions and other beliefs. It is only against this backdrop that the attempt to discredit a belief by calling attention to an atypical cause (e.g., a desire or fear) makes sense. If we were to discover that a hypochondriac's fear of illness strangely but nevertheless regularly caused true beliefs that ordinarily would be arrived at by apprehensions of and believings about the way the world is and logical relations, then we would be justified in presuming that future beliefs of this individual that are caused by this fear would be true. We would not, however, be justified in concluding that the beliefs of normal persons are not caused by apprehensions of and beliefs about the way the world is, logical relations, and other beliefs. We would simply but rightly conclude that it was weird or fluky that this hypochondriac had his beliefs formed in this odd way.

In conclusion, we want to make clear that we have not provided a decisive argument against strict naturalism. What we have argued is that if strict naturalism is true, then a belief that it is true cannot be causally explained by mental events (apprehensions and beliefs about the way the world is). Given strict naturalism, there cannot be mental-to-mental causation, and a belief that strict naturalism is true must have a causal explanation that is ultimately thoroughly nonmental in nature. Not only must this belief have this kind of explanation, so also must every one of our other true beliefs. That nonmental causes can produce all our true beliefs, among which are veritable hosts that are seemingly conclusions of arguments (chains of reasoning) involving mental-to-mental causation, is, dare we say, a coincidence of the highest magnitude. Indeed, it is a coincidence on the same scale as that which we pointed out in chapter 2: it would be as though all the movements of our fingers while typing this manuscript occurred but were not ultimately the effects of mental causes that have irreducible teleological explanations in the form of purposes. Though the magnitude of coincidence would be similar, we stress that the argument from reason is distinct from the argument put forth in chapter 2 in defense of teleological explanation of choices. As we understand matters, it is important to recognize that something's being a mental explanation is not sufficient for its being teleological in nature. Because a purpose is mental in nature, a choice's having a purposeful explanation is sufficient for its having a mental explanation, but having a mental explanation is not sufficient for having a purposeful explanation. This is because there are both purposeful mental explanations and nonpurposeful, causal mental explanations. Beliefs are mental events that have the latter kind of mental explanation.

Bibliography

Allport, Alan. 1988. "What Concept of Consciousness?" In *Consciousness in Contemporary Science,* edited by A. J. Marcel and E. Bisiach. Oxford: Oxford University Press.

Alston, William. 1991. *Perceiving God.* Ithaca, N.Y.: Cornell University Press.

Aquinas, Saint Thomas. 1975. *Summa Contra Gentiles, Book One: God.* Notre Dame, Ind.: University of Notre Dame Press.

Armstrong, David. 1978. "Naturalism, Materialism, and First Philosophy." *Philosophia* 8:261-76.

Bagger, Matthew. 1999. *Religious Experience, Justification, and History.* Cambridge: Cambridge University Press.

Bartlett, Thomas. 2005. "Black Freshmen Are More Religious Than Their Peers, Survey Finds." *Chronicle of Higher Education,* October 6.

————. 2006. "Professors Are More Religious Than Some Might Assume, Survey Finds." *Chronicle of Higher Education,* October 10.

Beilby, James. 2002. *Naturalism Defeated? Essays on Plantinga's Evolutionary Argument against Naturalism.* Ithaca, N.Y.: Cornell University Press.

Blackmore, Susan. 2006. *Conversations on Consciousness.* New York: Oxford University Press.

Broad, C. D. 1953. *Religion, Philosophy, and Psychical Research.* New York: Harcourt, Brace and Co.

Campbell, Keith. 1980. *Body and Mind.* Notre Dame, Ind.: University of Notre Dame Press.

Chalmers, David. 1996. *The Conscious Mind: In Search of a Fundamental Theory.* New York: Oxford University Press.

Chisholm, Roderick M. 1996. *A Realistic Theory of Categories: An Essay on Ontology.* Cambridge: Cambridge University Press.

Churchland, Paul M. 1995. *The Engine of Reason, the Seat of the Soul.* Cambridge, Mass., and London: MIT Press.

Craig, William Lane, and Quentin Smith. 1993. *Theism, Atheism, and Big Bang Cosmology.* Oxford: Clarendon.

Crick, Francis. 1994. *The Astonishing Hypothesis: The Scientific Search for the Soul.* New York: Scribner.

Danto, Arthur. 1967. "Naturalism." In *Encyclopedia of Philosophy,* edited by Paul Edwards. New York: Macmillan.

Darwin, Charles. 1898. *The Descent of Man.* London: John Murray.

———. 1969. *The Autobiography of Charles Darwin.* Edited by Nora Barlow. New York: Norton.

Dawkins, Richard. 1986. *The Blind Watchmaker: Why the Evidence of Evolution Reveals a Universe without Design.* New York: Norton.

———. 1989. *The Selfish Gene.* 2nd ed. Oxford: Oxford University Press.

———. 1995. *River out of Eden: A Darwinian View of Life.* London: Phoenix.

———. 1996. "A Survival Machine." In *The Third Culture,* edited by J. Brockman. New York: Simon and Schuster.

———. 2003. *A Devil's Chaplain.* London: Weidenfeld and Nicolson.

———. 2006. *The God Delusion.* Boston: Houghton Mifflin.

De Caro, Mario, and David Macarthur, eds. 2004. *Naturalism in Question.* Cambridge: Harvard University Press.

Dennett, Daniel. 1978. *Brainstorms: Philosophical Essays on Mind and Psychology.* Montgomery, Vt.: Bradford Books.

———. 1984. *Elbow Room.* Cambridge: MIT Press.

———. 1991. *Consciousness Explained.* Boston: Little, Brown.

———. 2000. "Facing Backwards on the Problem of Consciousness." In *Explaining Consciousness — the "Hard Problem."* Cambridge: MIT Press.

———. 2003. *Freedom Evolves.* New York: Viking Press.

———. 2006. *Breaking the Spell: Religion as a Natural Phenomenon.* New York: Viking Press.

Descartes, René. 1911. *The Philosophical Works of Descartes.* Vol. 1. Translated by Elizabeth S. Haldane and G. R. T. Ross. Cambridge: Cambridge University Press.

———. 1970. *Descartes: Philosophical Letters.* Edited and translated by Anthony Kenny. Oxford: Clarendon.

Dretske, Fred I. 1995. *Naturalizing the Mind.* Cambridge: MIT Press.

Everitt, Nicholas. 2004. *The Non-existence of God.* London: Routledge.

Feynman, Richard. 1998. *The Meaning of It All.* Reading, Mass.: Perseus Books.

Flanagan, Owen. 2002. *The Problem of the Soul.* New York: Basic Books.

Fodor, Jerry. 2002. "Is Science Biologically Possible?" In *Naturalism Defeated? Es-*

says on Plantinga's Evolutionary Argument against Naturalism, ed. James Beilby, pp. 30-42. Ithaca, N.Y.: Cornell University Press.

Foster, John. 1991. *The Immaterial Self: A Defense of the Cartesian Dualist Conception of the Mind*. New York: Routledge.

Frank, Caroline. 1989. *The Evidential Force of Religious Experience*. Oxford: Clarendon.

Futuyma, Douglas. 1982. *Science on Trial: The Case for Evolution*. New York: Pantheon Books.

Gellman, Jerome. 1997. *Experience of God and the Rationality of Theistic Belief*. Ithaca, N.Y.: Cornell University Press.

Georgalis, Nicholas. 2006. *The Primacy of the Subjective: Foundations for a Unified Theory of Mind and Language*. Cambridge: MIT Press.

Goetz, Stewart. 2003. "Theodicy." *Philosophia Christi* 5:459-84.

————. 2005. "Substance Dualism." In *In Search of the Soul*, edited by Joel B. Green and Stuart L. Palmer, pp. 33-60. Downers Grove, Ill.: InterVarsity.

Gray, Jeffrey A. 1995. "The Contents of Consciousness: A Neuropsychological Conjecture." *Behavioral and Brain Sciences* 18, no. 4: 659-722.

Hannay, Alastair. 1987. "The Claims of Consciousness: A Critical Survey." *Inquiry* 30:395-434.

Hasker, William. 1999. *The Emergent Self*. Ithaca, N.Y.: Cornell University Press.

Haught, John F. 2006. *Is Nature Enough? Meaning and Truth in the Age of Science*. New York: Cambridge University Press.

Hill, Daniel J. 2005. *Divinity and Maximal Greatness*. London: Routledge.

Hofstadter, Douglas. 1980. "Reductionism and Religion." Reply to John Searle. *Behavioral and Brain Sciences* 3:434.

Honderich, Ted. 1993. *How Free Are You? The Determinism Problem*. New York: Oxford University Press.

Hume, David. 1970. *Dialogues concerning Natural Religion*. Edited by N. Pike. Indianapolis: Bobbs-Merrill Educational.

————. 1978. *A Treatise of Human Nature*. Edited by L. A. Selby-Bigge. Oxford: Clarendon.

Jackson, Frank. 1982. "Epiphenomenal Qualia." *Philosophical Quarterly* 32:127-36.

Kane, Robert. 1999. "Responsibility, Luck, and Chance: Reflections on Free Will and Indeterminism." *Journal of Philosophy* 96:217-40.

Kenny, Anthony. 2006. *What I Believe*. London: Continuum International Publishing Group.

Kim, Jaegwon. 1996. *Philosophy of Mind*. Boulder, Colo.: Westview.

————. 1998. *Mind in a Physical World*. Cambridge: MIT Press.

————. 2002. "Book Symposia: *Mind in a Physical World*: Responses." *Philosophy and Phenomenological Research* 65:674-77.

————. 2005. *Physicalism, or Something Near Enough.* Princeton: Princeton University Press.

Kolata, Gina. 2007. "A Surprising Secret to a Long Life: Stay in School." *New York Times,* January 3.

Koons, Anthony. 2000. *Realism Regained.* Oxford: Oxford University Press.

Kornblith, Hilary. 1994. "Naturalism: Both Metaphysical and Epistemological." *Midwest Studies in Philosophy* 19:39-52.

Kretzman, Norman. 1997. *The Metaphysics of Theism.* Oxford: Clarendon.

Leslie, John. 2001. *Infinite Minds: A Philosophical Theology.* Oxford: Oxford University Press.

Lewis, C. S. 1960. *Miracles.* 2nd ed. New York: Macmillan.

Lockwood, Michael. 2003. "Consciousness and the Quantum Worlds." In *Consciousness: New Philosophical Perspectives,* edited by Q. Smith and A. Jokric. Oxford: Clarendon.

Loewer, Barry. 2001. Review of *Mind in a Physical World: An Essay on the Mind-Body Problem and Mental Causation,* by Jaegwon Kim. *Journal of Philosophy* 98:315-24.

Madell, Geoffrey. 1988. *Mind and Materialism.* Edinburgh: Edinburgh University Press.

————. 2003. "Materialism and the First Person." In *Minds and Persons: Royal Institute of Philosophy Supplement,* edited by Anthony O'Hear, pp. 123-40. Cambridge: Cambridge University Press.

Mann, William E. 2005. "Divine Sovereignty and Aseity." In *The Oxford Handbook of Philosophy of Religion,* edited by William J. Wainwright, pp. 35-58. Oxford: Oxford University Press.

Manson, Neil A., ed. 2003. *God and Design: The Teleological Argument and Modern Science.* London: Routledge.

McDermott, Drew. 2001. *Mind and Mechanism.* Cambridge: MIT Press.

McGinn, Colin. 1991. *The Problem of Consciousness.* Oxford: Blackwell.

————. 1999. *The Mysterious Flame: Conscious Minds in a Material World.* New York: Basic Books.

McGrath, Alister. 2005. *Dawkins' God: Genes, Memes, and the Meaning of Life.* Oxford: Blackwell.

Melnyk, Andrew. 2007. "A Case for Physicalism about the Human Mind." Available at http://www.infidels.org/library/modern/andrew_melnyk/physicalism.html.

Minsky, Marvin. 1985. *The Society of Mind.* New York: Simon and Schuster.

Moreland, James Porter. 2001. *Universals, Qualities, and Quality-Instances.* Montreal: McGill-Queen's University Press.

Nagel, Ernest. 1958. "Naturalism Reconsidered." In *Essays in Philosophy,* edited by H. Peterson. New York: Washington Square Press.

Nagel, Thomas. 1979. *Mortal Question.* Cambridge: Cambridge University Press.

————. 1986. *The View from Nowhere.* Oxford: Oxford University Press.

————. 1998. "Conceiving the Impossible and the Mind-Body Problem." *Philosophy* 73:337-52.

Narveson, Jan. 2003. "God by Design?" In *God and Design: The Teleological Argument and Modern Science,* edited by Neil A. Manson, pp. 88-104. London: Routledge.

Needham, Rodney. 1972. *Belief, Language, and Experience.* Chicago: University of Chicago Press.

Nielsen, Kai. 1996. *Naturalism without Foundations.* Buffalo: Prometheus Books.

————. 1997. "Naturalistic Explanations of Theistic Belief." In *A Companion to Philosophy of Religion,* edited by P. Quinn and C. Taliaferro, pp. 402-9. Oxford: Blackwell.

O'Hear, Anthony. 2002. *Beyond Evolution: Human Nature and the Limits of Evolutionary Explanation.* Oxford: Oxford University Press.

O'Shaughnessy, Brian. 1980. *The Will: A Dual Aspect Theory.* New York: Cambridge University Press.

Overbye, Dennis. 2007. "Free Will: Now You Have It, Now You Don't." *New York Times,* January 2.

Papineau, David. 1993. *Philosophical Naturalism.* Oxford: Blackwell.

————. 2002. *Thinking about Consciousness.* Oxford: Oxford University Press.

Penfield, Wilder. 1975. *The Mystery of the Mind.* Princeton: Princeton University Press.

Penguin Dictionary of Philosophy, The. 1997. Rev. ed. London and New York: Penguin Books.

Perry, John. 2001. *Knowledge, Possibility, and Consciousness.* Cambridge: MIT Press.

Phillips, D. Z. 2005a. *The Problem of Evil and the Problem of God.* Minneapolis: Fortress.

————. 2005b. "Wittgensteinianism: Logic, Reality, and God." In *The Oxford Handbook of Philosophy of Religion,* edited by William J. Wainwright, pp. 447-71. Oxford: Oxford University Press.

Pollack, Andrew. 2004. "With Tiny Brain Implants, Just Thinking May Make It So." *New York Times,* April 13.

————. 2006. "Paralyzed Man Uses Thoughts to Move a Cursor." *New York Times,* July 13.

Popper, Karl, and John C. Eccles. 1977. *The Self and Its Brain.* New York: Routledge.

Post, John. 1991. *Metaphysics: A Contemporary Introduction.* New York: Paragon.

Pruss, Alexander. 2006. *The Principle of Sufficient Reason.* Cambridge: Cambridge University Press.

Quinn, Philip. 1997. "Tiny Selves: Chisholm on the Simplicity of the Soul." In *The Philosophy of Roderick M. Chisholm,* edited by Lewis Edwin Hahn, pp. 55-67. Chicago: Open Court.

Quinton, Anthony. 1973. *The Nature of Things.* London: Routledge and Kegan Paul.

Reid, Thomas. 1969. *Essays on the Active Powers of the Human Mind.* Cambridge: MIT Press.

—————. 1975. "Of Identity." In *Personal Identity,* edited by John Perry, pp. 107-12. Berkeley: University of California Press.

Rey, Georges. 1997. *Contemporary Philosophy of Mind.* Oxford: Blackwell.

Rolston, Holmes, III. 1999. *Genes, Genesis, and God.* Cambridge: Cambridge University Press.

Rorty, Richard. 1965. "Mind-Body Identity." *Review of Metaphysics* 19:24-54.

Rowe, William. 1975. *The Cosmological Argument.* Princeton: Princeton University Press.

—————. 2004. *Can God Be Free?* Oxford: Oxford University Press.

Rundle, Bede. 2004. *Why There Is Something Rather Than Nothing.* New York: Clarendon.

Ruse, M., and E. O. Wilson. 1986. "Moral Philosophy as Applied Science." *Philosophy* 61:173-92.

Russell, Bertrand. 1957. *Why I Am Not a Christian.* London: Unwin.

—————. 1961. *Religion and Science.* Oxford: Oxford University Press.

Russell, Bertrand, and F. C. Copleston. 1964. "The Existence of God." In *The Existence of God,* p. 175. Problems of Philosophy Series. New York: Macmillan.

Sagan, Carl. 1980. *Cosmos.* New York: Random House.

Searle, John. 1992. *The Rediscovery of the Mind.* Cambridge: MIT Press.

—————. 1997. *The Mystery of Consciousness.* New York: New York Review of Books.

—————. 2004. *Mind: A Brief Introduction.* New York: Oxford University Press.

Sellars, Roy Wood. 1922. *Evolutionary Naturalism.* Chicago: Open Court.

Sosa, Ernest. 1984. "Mind-Body Interaction and Supervenient Causation." In *Midwest Studies in Philosophy,* vol. 9, edited by Peter A. French, Theodore E. Uehling, Jr., and Howard K. Wettstein, pp. 271-81. Minneapolis: University of Minnesota Press.

Stenmark, Mikael. 2001. *Scientism: Science, Ethics, and Religion.* Aldershot: Ashgate.

Stroud, Barry. 2004. "The Charm of Naturalism." In *Naturalism in Question,* edited by Mario De Caro and David Macarthur. Cambridge: Harvard University Press.

Stubenberg, Leopold. 1998. *Consciousness and Qualia.* Amsterdam and Philadelphia: John Benjamins Publishing Co.

Stump, Eleanore. 1982. "Theology and Physics in *De sacramento altaris:* Ockham's Theory of Indivisibles." In *Infinity and Continuity in Ancient and Medieval Thought,* edited by Norman Kretzman, pp. 207-30. Ithaca, N.Y.: Cornell University Press.

Swinburne, Richard. 1991. *The Existence of God.* Oxford: Oxford University Press.

—————. 1996. *Is There a God?* Oxford: Oxford University Press.

Taliaferro, Charles. 1994. *Consciousness and the Mind of God.* Cambridge: Cambridge University Press.

——. 1997. "Possibilities in the Philosophy of Mind." *Philosophy and Phenomenological Research* 57:127-37.

——. 1998. *Contemporary Philosophy of Religion.* Malden, Mass.: Blackwell.

——. 2002. "Sensibility and Possibilia: A Defense of Thought Experiments." *Philosophia Christi.*

——. 2005. *Evidence and Faith.* Cambridge: Cambridge University Press.

Taylor, Charles. 1989. *Sources of the Self.* Cambridge: Cambridge University Press.

Taylor, Richard. 1974. *Metaphysics.* 2nd ed. Englewood Cliffs, N.J.: Prentice-Hall.

Teske, Roland. 2001. "Augustine's Theory of the Soul." In *The Cambridge Companion to Augustine,* edited by Eleonore Stump and Norman Kretzman, pp. 116-23. Cambridge: Cambridge University Press.

Unger, Peter. 2006. *All the Power in the World.* Oxford: Oxford University Press.

Ward, Keith. 1996. *God, Chance, and Necessity.* Oxford: Oneworld.

Wilson, Edward O. 1978. *On Human Nature.* Cambridge: Harvard University Press.

Woons, Robert. 2000. *Realism Regained.* Oxford: Oxford University Press.

Wynn, Mark. 1999. *God and Goodness: A Natural Theological Perspective.* London: Routledge.

Zahavi, Dan. 2005. *Subjectivity and Selfhood: Investigating the First-Person Perspective.* Cambridge: MIT Press.

Index